D1560104

**Insight Study Guide**

Timothy Roberts

# Jane Eyre

## Charlotte Brontë

insight

**insight**

*Charlotte Brontë's Jane Eyre* by Timothy Roberts
Insight Study Guide series

Copyright © 2011 Insight Publications Pty Ltd

First published in 2011 by
Insight Publications Pty Ltd
ABN 57 005 102 983
89 Wellington Street
St Kilda VIC 3182
Australia
Tel: +61 3 9523 0044
Fax: +61 3 9523 2044
Email: books@insightpublications.com
Website: www.insightpublications.com

This edition published in 2011 in the United States of America by
Insight Publications Pty Ltd, Australia.

ISBN-13: 978-1-921411-84-7

Library of Congress Control Number: 2011931342

Cover Design by The Modern Art Production Group
Cover Illustrations by The Modern Art Production Group,
istockphoto* and House Industries
Internal Design by Sarn Potter

Printed in the United States of America by Lightning Source
10 9 8 7 6 5 4 3 2 1

# contents

# CHARACTER MAP

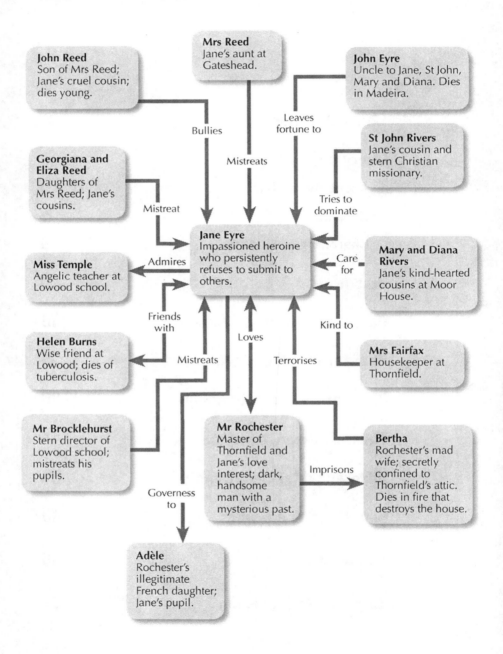

**John Reed**
Son of Mrs Reed; Jane's cruel cousin; dies young.

**Mrs Reed**
Jane's aunt at Gateshead.

**John Eyre**
Uncle to Jane, St John, Mary and Diana. Dies in Madeira.

**Georgiana and Eliza Reed**
Daughters of Mrs Reed; Jane's cousins.

**St John Rivers**
Jane's cousin and stern Christian missionary.

*Bullies*

*Leaves fortune to*

*Mistreats*

*Mistreat*

*Tries to dominate*

**Jane Eyre**
Impassioned heroine who persistently refuses to submit to others.

**Miss Temple**
Angelic teacher at Lowood school.

*Admires*

*Care for*

**Mary and Diana Rivers**
Jane's kind-hearted cousins at Moor House.

*Friends with*

*Loves*

*Kind to*

**Helen Burns**
Wise friend at Lowood; dies of tuberculosis.

*Mistreats*

*Terrorises*

**Mrs Fairfax**
Housekeeper at Thornfield.

**Mr Brocklehurst**
Stern director of Lowood school; mistreats his pupils.

**Mr Rochester**
Master of Thornfield and Jane's love interest; dark, handsome man with a mysterious past.

*Imprisons*

**Bertha**
Rochester's mad wife; secretly confined to Thornfield's attic. Dies in fire that destroys the house.

*Governess to*

**Adèle**
Rochester's illegitimate French daughter; Jane's pupil.

# OVERVIEW

## About the author

Charlotte Brontë (1816–1855) was a member of one of history's most extraordinary literary families. The third of six children, Charlotte's genius, along with that of her sisters Emily (1818–1848) and Anne (1820–1849), has been celebrated since the initial publication of their works.

The family was marred by tragedy: Charlotte's mother died in 1821, the year after the birth of Charlotte's youngest sister Anne, and the Brontës were subsequently raised by their father. All of the Brontë children were to die at a young age.

Charlotte's early childhood was relatively happy. The five sisters and their only brother, Branwell, spent their youth at the family home, 'The Parsonage', in the town of Haworth. Charlotte and her sisters' formative experience was their appalling tenure at the Clergy Daughters' School. Their wayward brother Branwell stayed at The Parsonage during this time, being educated by his father and generally getting up to mischief. Charlotte, however, was sent to boarding school when she was just eight, and witnessed the cruelty and deprivation that she would later draw on so vividly in the unforgettable early chapters of *Jane Eyre*. The Clergy Daughters' School was fictionalised as 'Lowood'.

Although the Brontë girls only attended the school for less than a year, its terrible conditions took their toll on two of the sisters, Maria (1814–1825) and Elizabeth (1815–1825), who both died after being sent home from school in ill-health, aged only eleven and ten. By the time she was nine years old, Charlotte had already lost two of her four sisters – a situation which we, used to modern medicine and protecting children from all forms of harm, would find utterly shocking today.

After Maria and Elizabeth's deaths in 1825, the surviving Brontë sisters were brought home to the Parsonage, where they wrote literary fantasies with their brother Branwell. Together, they transcribed their remarkable stories into tiny books, written in miniscule font to protect them from adults' prying eyes. Their sagas, the manuscripts of which survive today, 'demonstrate the increasing skill, developing assurance and new interests of the gifted young writer [Charlotte] as she experiments with various genres and narrative techniques.' (Alexander 2005, p.vii)

As their father was of limited means, however, this peaceful interlude could not last forever. In 1835, aged 19, Charlotte was sent to Roe Head to work as a governess until 1838 – an experience which also inspired part of the plot of *Jane Eyre*. Longing to escape from the stifling environment, she bitterly described her experience at Roe Head as one of 'wretched bondage' (2001:404). Charlotte coped by maintaining a rich fantasy life during her time as a governess.

Following her stint at Roe Head, Charlotte and her sister Emily – both with ambitions to start a school of their own – were sent on a funded study trip to Brussels. Charlotte's time there was again unhappy: she had fallen in love with her tutor, who was a married man. She returned to the Parsonage in 1844, later drawing on her experience in Brussels for her novel *Villette*, about a student's unrequited love for her teacher.

After unsuccessfully attempting to establish a school with Emily and Anne, Charlotte published a book of the sisters' poems in 1846. As this venture proved unsuccessful, only selling two copies, the sisters decided to try their hand at writing novels. After the publisher's rejection of Charlotte's first novel, *The Professor*, *Jane Eyre* was published with success in 1847. (Anne and Emily's novels, *Agnes Grey* and *Wuthering Heights*, were also published in the same year.) The sisters' novels can be seen as sophisticated precursors of today's simplistic 'romantic fiction', which often centres on the 'dark handsome stranger' template perfected by the Brontë sisters.

As the sisters were worried about the public's reaction to overly passionate novels written by women, they took on the pseudonyms 'Currer Bell' (Charlotte), 'Ellis Bell' (Emily) and 'Acton Bell' (Anne). Their three novels, particularly *Jane Eyre*, met with considerable success. At this stage, public and publisher alike assumed that the sisters' novels had been written by men.

This changed in 1848, when Charlotte, Emily and Anne met their publisher in London and revealed their identities. After this revelation, the sisters were introduced into London society and taken to cultural and literary events.

This relatively happy period was cut short, however, when the Brontës learned of their brother Branwell's illness. A dissolute and somewhat tyrannical character (perhaps the inspiration for the character of John Reed in *Jane Eyre*), Branwell had lapsed into alcoholism and drug addiction in his later life. He succumbed to tuberculosis in July, followed in December by the perennially sickly Emily. Charlotte's remaining sister, Anne, died of the same disease six months later.

Now the only surviving sibling, Charlotte threw herself vigorously into her work. Her publication of *Shirley* in 1849 again gave her the opportunity to mix with famous writers and artists in London – most notably the novelist William Makepeace Thackeray, to whom *Jane Eyre* is dedicated.

Charlotte's final sombre masterpiece, *Villette*, was published in 1853; drawing on her experience in Brussels several years before, it relates the story of a naive young woman who becomes obsessed with her charismatic French teacher. *Villette*, which draws heavily on the elements of alienation and loneliness prevalent in Gothic literature, stands today as a macabre companion piece to *Jane Eyre*. It explores the dark and destructive side of human love, just as *Jane Eyre* explores its passion and promise.

Charlotte was not alone during this time. After rejecting an offer of marriage from the Reverend Arthur Nicholls due to her father's disapproval, Charlotte finally assented to marry him in 1854. She became pregnant with her first child soon after. Like so much else in the Brontës' lives, this happiness was only fleeting. Aged only 39, Charlotte died from complications during the pregnancy on 31 March 1855. Tragically, her father outlived all six of his children.

## Synopsis

*Jane Eyre* is the story of an impoverished and downtrodden orphan girl's difficult path toward prosperity, love and acceptance. Beginning life as an unwanted child in the care of her uncaring aunt and sadistic cousin, Jane undergoes a number of gruelling personal trials before finally finding true happiness as the wife of the dark, handsome and mysterious Mr Rochester.

After fighting back against her aunt's cruelty, Jane is despatched to an appalling boarding school named Lowood. Her only consolation during her first years there is the time she spends with two friends: the compassionate Miss Temple, a teacher; and the beautiful, doomed student Helen Burns, who dies from consumption (tuberculosis). While Jane herself is spared, many other schoolgirls perish in a typhus epidemic.

Although things improve at Lowood after the outbreak, Jane longs for escape. After several more years (both as a student and teacher) at the school, she advertises and is hired as a governess. Jane leaves Lowood for Thornfield, her new employer's house.

Jane soon meets the master of Thornfield, one Mr Rochester, and becomes the governess of Adèle, his illegitimate French-speaking daughter. Rochester is antagonistic and dismissive toward Jane, displaying an unreliable temper which leaves the heroine unsure of whether he likes or hates her. As Rochester and Jane gradually spend more time together, she begins to fall in love with him. She also learns that Adèle is Rochester's love-child with a Parisian mistress.

Their developing relationship is a troubled one. Firstly, Thornfield seems haunted by a malign spirit, which enters Rochester's room and attempts to burn him to death. After Jane saves his life, she suspects the servant, Grace Poole, is responsible for the incident.

Jane is dismayed to find out that Rochester intends to marry the wealthy and unpleasant Blanche Ingram. While a party of guests are staying at Thornfield, Rochester dresses up as a fortune-teller in order to extract an admission of love from Jane, leaving her further puzzled about his feelings for her. Before the two can reconcile, Rochester is dismayed to find out that a man named Mason has come to Thornfield. During the night, Mason is brutally attacked – presumably by Grace Poole, the same servant who earlier was suspected of attempting to burn Rochester in his sleep. Jane is assigned to tend to Mason's wounds, but he departs early the next morning, leaving many questions unanswered.

Jane takes leave from Thornfield to attend the deathbed of her aunt, who reveals that she still deeply resents Jane for her childhood outbursts, and also that Jane has an uncle who wished to adopt her. After her aunt's death, Jane eagerly returns to Thornfield and Mr Rochester.

Rochester eventually reveals that his courtship of Blanche Ingram was in fact a sham designed to arouse Jane's jealousy. He professes his love for Jane, and the two become engaged. Jane's new-found happiness comes to an abrupt end on her wedding-day when Mason and his lawyer reveal Rochester's darkest secret: he is already married. Rochester admits his crime and reveals that his insane wife, Bertha, is imprisoned in Thornfield's attic – it was she, not Grace Poole, who was responsible for the destructive events at Thornfield. On learning of the madwoman's existence, Jane leaves Rochester and flees to a distant village.

Utterly alone, Jane is forced to sleep in the open and beg for food before being taken in by the kindly sisters, Diana and Mary Rivers. Their brother St John, however, is a stern Christian missionary who remains cold toward Jane, although he is able to find her employment as a school teacher. In order to remain hidden from Mr Rochester, Jane gives him a false name.

When St John glimpses Jane's real name on a piece of artwork, he realises that she is in fact his (and his sisters') cousin. St John informs Jane of this connection and reveals that their mutual uncle has left her a large fortune. Jane, delighted to have relatives at last, vows to share the money equally between them. She and her three cousins live peacefully together until St John attempts to use his powerful but cold personality to coerce Jane into a loveless marriage and exile to India. Jane is on the verge of accepting when she hears Rochester's faint voice, calling to her.

Taking this as a sign, Jane returns to Thornhill only to discover it has burnt to the ground since her departure. Rochester, blinded and crippled by the blaze, is living miserably at Ferndean, his second home. His mad wife Bertha was killed in the conflagration. Jane hastens to Ferndean, where she and Rochester are finally married.

## Character Summaries

### Jane Eyre

**Key quote**

'I am glad you are no relation of mine: I will never call you aunt again as long as I live.' (p.44)

Jane is a surprisingly complex character. At first, she seems to be a rather demure, fragile young girl who suffers silently at the hands of her aunt, her cousin, and her teachers. Yet there is a barely-repressed element of anger within Jane that fuels her throughout her life and, at major moments in the novel, leads to passionate outbursts. She always refuses to compromise on her principles – decisively rejecting, for example, St John's loveless offer of marriage – and steadily works her way toward her goal of marrying her true love, Rochester. Throughout her trials, Jane retains her passionate and intense characteristics.

### Mrs Reed & Master Reed

**Key quotes**

**Master Reed:** 'You have no business to take our books; you are a dependent, mamma says; you have no money; your father left you none; you ought to beg, and not to live here with gentlemen's children like us ...' (p.13)

**Mrs Reed:** 'Take her away to the red-room, and lock her in there.' (p.14)

Jane's guardian and her son at Gateshead are spiteful individuals with no redeeming characteristics. Master Reed is a sadistic bully who is pampered and spoiled by his indulgent mother, and Jane suffers at the hands of both. Jane carries her rage at this maltreatment with her to Lowood, but learns forgiveness as she grows older.

### Mr Brocklehurst

**Key quote**

'... this girl, who might be one of God's own lambs, is a little castaway – not a member of the true flock, but evidently an interloper and an alien.' (p.78)

Brontë's most blatant representative of patriarchy, Brocklehurst is a fearsome presence in Jane's life. At first awed by his grim character and imposing presence, Jane soon discovers Brocklehurst's passion for exercising unrestrained cruelty on Lowood's students. Brocklehurst is similar in appearance to Rochester, yet lacks all of his redeeming characteristics.

### Mr Rochester

**Key quote**

'Then you condemn me to live wretched, and to die accursed?' (p.364)

A perfect image of the 'tall, dark and handsome' hero, the haughty and aristocratic Rochester is Jane's opposite in many ways. He certainly sees himself as 'above' Jane, until his class-based prejudices are conquered by love. He evidently enjoys matching wits with Jane, appreciating her intelligence, honesty and principles.

Jane rejects Rochester when she finds out that he is already married. She pines for him when they are separated yet refuses to become his mistress. The death of Bertha clears the way for Jane to return to Rochester and marry him. A deeply flawed hero, Rochester learns humility and manages to overcome the more negative aspects of his personality after being severely injured in the fire.

### Adèle

**Key quote**

'Est-ce que je ne puis pas prendre une seule de ces fleurs magnifiques, mademoiselle?' ('May I take just one of those magnificent flowers, miss?') (p.198)

Adèle, Rochester's illegitimate child, is the result of his affair with a Parisian opera-girl. Obsessed with appearances and trivialities, Adèle is utterly unlike Jane and Rochester. In many ways, Adèle is the personification of the shallowness that Jane goes to such lengths to reject.

### St John Rivers

**Key quote**

'You shall be mine: I claim you – not for my pleasure, but for my Sovereign's service.' (p.464)

St John, the novel's other love interest, at first appears to be Jane's 'perfect match'. Pure of heart and filled with missionary zeal, this passionless, dominating man attempts to coerce Jane into marrying him and travelling to India to work as a missionary. Although attracted to the idea of mission work, Jane refuses on the grounds that it would be a loveless marriage.

A repressed, sexually neutered and deeply masochistic individual, St John gives up any possibility of human happiness in order to fulfil what he sees as his 'calling'. Rejecting his offer of marriage is therefore one of Jane's most sensible acts.

### Bertha

**Key quote**

'Ha! Ha!' (p.130)

Bertha, the mad and extremely dangerous inhabitant of Thornfield's attic, is Rochester's first wife. She represents all forms of depravity and wretchedness. When Bertha's madness reveals itself after their marriage in the West Indies, Rochester takes her back to England and conceals her from public view. Bertha eventually perishes after throwing herself from the flaming roof of Thornfield.

# BACKGROUND & CONTEXT

Today, *Jane Eyre* – along with Emily Brontë's *Wuthering Heights* – stands as one of the undisputed masterpieces of English literature. Charlotte Brontë created an intensely passionate, heavily romantic vocabulary that further extended the novel's possibilities, fusing the overarching emotions of Romantic poetry with convincing literary realism.

*Jane Eyre* is also a cornerstone of feminist literature. In her study, *A Literature of Their Own*, Elaine Showalter aptly called Jane 'the heroine of fulfilment' (1977, p.112). In a period when literary heroines were often passive individuals destined to take their place as obedient wives and mothers, Brontë dared to create a character who represented the very antithesis (opposite) of these ideals: utterly spontaneous, incredibly headstrong and indomitably strong-willed, Jane is unique. Perhaps Rochester's own assessment of Jane's character – 'never was anything at once so frail and so indomitable' (p.366) – sums her up most concisely. As Rochester observed, Jane always seems to be at the mercy of others, yet she always gets her own way in the end. Charlotte's assault on the gender ideals of her day was concealed by her dramatic language, but *Jane Eyre* is no less forceful for that.

There had been strong-willed female characters in English Literature before *Jane Eyre* – such as Becky Sharp, the protagonist of Thackeray's *Vanity Fair* – but these were almost always 'evil' in some way or another: Becky's dominating ways, for example, cause immeasurable harm to others. Jane, conversely, is both sexually assertive *and* morally pure, a combination that was highly unusual in an age when female desire was almost invariably seen as sinful. For this reason, Jane is one of the key precursors to the admirable female characters who populate modern literature. While Brontë's explicitly feminist contemporaries Harriet Martineau and Mary Wollstonecraft wrote explicit polemics defending the rights of women, Brontë's work had the advantage of reaching beyond a select literary audience to truly influence a mass audience.

Yet the novel's importance goes beyond its social effects. On a purely literary level, Brontë's characters are utterly indelible. Her ability to convey people's inhumanity as well as deep compassion demonstrates a huge and virtually unequalled emotional range. Brocklehurst's savage inhumanity, Mrs Reed's ice-cold detachment,

John Reed's violent depravity and St John's overweening arrogance all characterise unforgettable villains (or, in St John's case, hero-villains). Rochester's painful narrative of redemption, Helen Burns' slow and tragic decline and death, and – above all else – Jane's own tortured path to true happiness are equally resonant. By fusing the fictional world of fantasy with the realist novel's keen sense of moral outrage and social awareness, Charlotte Brontë stands alone as a unique figure in the crowded pantheon of nineteenth-century English literature.

# GENRE, STRUCTURE & LANGUAGE

## Genre

### The romance novel

*Jane Eyre*, along with Jane Austen's *Pride and Prejudice*, is one of the most famous romance novels of all time. But while Austen focuses on civilised society and behaviour, Brontë is more concerned with the extreme states such as passion, cruelty and terror. Both novels are based on a central theme of the romance plot: the heroine's gradual humanisation of the gruff hero (Darcy in *Pride and Prejudice* and Rochester in *Jane Eyre*).

Like many romances, *Jane Eyre* portrays a woman's struggle between two men: the passionate yet erratic Rochester and the rational yet controlling St John Rivers. To decide, Jane is forced to choose between her passion and her reason.

Jane's second love interest, St John, possesses the refinement and gentility that Rochester lacks. Yet St John's refusal to respect her heart's wishes repulses Jane. When Jane and Rochester reunite, their personalities – like Elizabeth's and Darcy's at the conclusion of *Pride and Prejudice* – finally harmonise.

### The Gothic novel

For a supposedly romantic book, *Jane Eyre* contains a surprising amount of horror. The Gothic tale has been defined as a narrative that will 'almost certainly offend classical tastes and rational principles' (Baldick 1992, p.xiii) – and Brontë's novel certainly did that upon publication.

Many potentially disturbing elements of Jane's personality are concealed, yet her assertive nature still disturbs many people. For example, her aunt is traumatised for life by Jane's savage childhood outburst, and dies wondering 'how for nine years you could be patient and quiescent under any treatment, and in the tenth break out all fire and violence ...' (p.276).

Jane's violent streak seems almost demonic at times. This split nature connects her to the 'monster' figure that haunts Gothic literature. Jane, like the Gothic monster, presents a genuine challenge to the norms of her society.

Many characters struggle to understand their deep misgivings about Jane. Brocklehurst succinctly expresses the unsettling discrepancy between Jane's outer passivity and her inner aggression:

> ... no signal deformity points her out as a marked character.
> Who would think that the Evil One had already found a servant
> and agent in her? (p.78)

The 'concealed' nature of Jane's demonic personality subtly aligns her with another famous Victorian monster: Mr Hyde, from Robert Louis Stevenson's *The Strange Case of Dr Jekyll & Mr Hyde*. As one character notes:

> He must be deformed somewhere; he gives a strong feeling
> of deformity, although I couldn't specify the point. (Stevenson
> 1979, p.34)

*Jane Eyre* can therefore be said to contain two 'monsters': the overt (Bertha) and the covert (Jane). Jane and Bertha's affinities are clearest in the following scene:

> ... presently she took my veil from its place ... she threw it over
> her own head, and turned to the mirror. At that moment I saw
> the reflection of the visage and features quite distinctly in the
> dark oblong glass ... she thrust up her candle close to my face ...
> I was aware her lurid visage flamed over mine ... (pp.346–347)

The boundaries between Jane and Bertha are blurred: for example, when Jane looks in the mirror, she sees Bertha's reflection; Bertha wears Jane's gown; the candle is brought up to Jane's face, but Bertha blows it out. As victims of a patriarchal system, Jane and Bertha have far more in common than it may seem.

When Jane sees Bertha a final time, her earlier empathy has vanished:

> The maniac bellowed: she parted her shaggy locks from her
> visage, and gazed wildly at her visitors. I recognised well that
> purple face – those bloated features. (p.338)

Bertha's reduction to a pathetic and pitiable individual makes Jane, who can successfully conceal her anger, arguably a far more powerful 'monstrous' figure than Bertha.

### The Bildungsroman

The *Bildungsroman*, a German word meaning 'novel of development' emerged in eighteenth-century Germany and has remained popular since. Many *Bildungsroman* narratives, including *Jane Eyre*, involve a 'rags-to-riches' plot charting a disadvantaged character's path to success.

Although *Jane Eyre* follows roughly the same structure as other *Bildungsroman* novels, it differs in a crucial respect: the story does not end with Jane's inheritance. Her financially secure position, while welcome, is not an end in itself: love, not money, is the novel's governing force.

### The moral allegory

*Jane Eyre* is tightly structured around the specific locations of Gateshead, Lowood, Thornfield, Millcote and Ferndean. Each place represents a different stage of Jane's development, as Brontë's physical world is *symbolic* as well as realistic. The novel's locations, described in convincing detail, reflect the protagonist's inner needs and desires.

This symbolic use of space is often seen in the 'moral allegory' or fable, the most famous being John Bunyan's *The Pilgrim's Progress* (1678). The narrator, Christian, undergoes a series of religious trials, and the locations he finds himself in – including 'The City of Destruction' and 'The Slough of Despond' – represent human temptations. Bunyan's landscape is *allegorical* – that is, its surface detail has a deeper meaning.

Critic Sandra Gilbert observed the symbolic importance of each location in *Jane Eyre*. Jane must overcome 'oppression (at Gateshead), starvation (at Lowood), madness (at Thornfield), and coldness (at Marsh End)' (2001, pp.483–4). At the deepest level, the terrain of *Jane Eyre* reflects Jane's own soul. Jane's earthy and natural final destination, Ferndean, suggests that her vision of happiness is located on earth with Rochester, not in heaven with St John.

# Structure

### Chronological structure

The narrative covers just over a decade of Jane's life, up to the age of 20. The final chapter is narrated ten years later, which would make the narrator around 30.

The time-scheme, however, is not evenly distributed. Jane is ten when her story begins, and Chapters 1–15 cover eight years at Lowood. The rest of the narrative – excluding the final chapter – takes place over a far shorter period.

Brontë often telescopes large timespans into a few pages. For example, the beginning of Chapter VII skips over 'January, February, and part of March' (p.71), and the narrator raises the issue of chronology:

> To the first ten years of my life I have given almost as many chapters. But this is not to be a regular autobiography: I am only bound to invoke memory where I know her responses will possess some degree of interest; therefore I now pass a space of almost eight years in silence ... (p.99)

The chronology therefore responds to Jane's own interests: important events are described in great detail, while unimportant ones are skipped over. Like its locations, the novel's time scheme reflects Jane's desires.

## Self-reflexivity

*Jane Eyre*'s surprisingly modern narrator often draws attention to the fact that she is telling a story. Most obviously, she refers directly to the 'reader' 34 times – 'Reader, I married him' (p.517) being the most famous.

Jane also often draws attention to her story's written nature:

> A new chapter in a novel is something like a new scene in a play; and when I draw up the curtain this time, reader, you must fancy you see a room in the George Inn at Millcote ... (p.111)

Brontë's use of this technique is interesting. On the one hand, having the character address the reader so often draws attention to the book as a *related story*, not as a natural sequence of events. By doing this, Brontë brings the reader closer to Jane's character, as well as highlighting the story's 'fairy tale' aspects.

## Shifting perspectives

Because Jane ages considerably during the novel, the novel's perspective subtly develops. Here is the adult narrator describing the feelings of her childhood self:

> What a consternation of soul was mine that dreary afternoon! How all my brain was in tumult, and all my heart in insurrection! Yet in what darkness, what dense ignorance, was the mental battle fought! I could not answer the ceaseless inward question – why I suffered; now, at the distance of – I will not say how many years – I see it clearly. (p.19)

This passage draws attention to the contrast between adult narrator and child character, because the narrator highlights the limitations of her younger self.

Elsewhere, though, the narrator describes the child's actions and feelings without glossing, as follows:

> My heart beat thick, my head grew hot; a sound filled my ears, which I deemed the rushing of wings ... (p.21)

Notice the difference between the two passages. The former reinterprets the child's feelings through an adult lens; the latter describes the *child's* thoughts and feelings without further explanation. Also, as the character's and narrator's age converge, explanatory passages become increasingly unnecessary.

### Flashbacks and premonitions

The story's linear structure is punctuated by a series of flashbacks which provide us with more information about past events.

The most important flashbacks are Rochester's recounting of his past life (pp.336–339 and pp.351–363). As we only have access to Jane's first-person perspective, the flashbacks represent Rochester's only chance to increase his hold on Jane's sympathy.

His first (brief) flashback takes place immediately after Jane's discovery of Bertha's existence (p.338). While he attempts to 'sell himself' to Jane by recounting his unhappy past, Rochester's initial efforts to justify his behaviour are unsuccessful. His second attempt at defending himself through a flashback (pp.351–363), however, does make him more sympathetic.

Flashbacks are just as useful in generating suspense. For instance, by concealing Bertha's true identity from the reader for as long as possible, the narrator can delay the bombshell of Rochester's history, which we only learn in flashback. The revelation is further delayed by the 'red herring' of Grace Poole, whom Rochester continues to blame for Bertha's actions.

Yet Rochester's second flashback is not enough to sway Jane. With the words, 'Mr Rochester, I will *not* be yours', Jane rejects his attempts to gain her sympathy and asserts her right to exist as an independent woman.

Another important flashback, related by an innkeeper (pp.490–495), explains the occurrences at Thornfield after Jane's departure. Suspense is again heightened, as the man keeps Jane (and the reader) on tenterhooks until she finally learns that Rochester is still living.

Mrs Reed's flashback about Jane on her deathbed (pp.266–7) explains her hatred; while her second flashback (pp.274–6) explains Jane's link to her uncle. Both flashbacks place Jane's life story in context by providing us with important new information.

Jane often experiences 'flash-forwards' or premonitions, which either anticipate what is to come, or provide a cryptic comment on her current life.

For example, Jane's 'dream of an infant, which I sometimes hushed in my arms, sometimes dandled on my knee, sometimes watched playing with daisies on a lawn, or again, dabbling its hands in running water' (p.254), which recurs throughout the novel, serves as a symbol of her own longing for protection and companionship, although Jane interprets the dream as a bad omen.

### The detective story

*Jane Eyre* can also be read as a detective story, in which Jane must unravel the mystery of Thornfield. In many ways, the novel's meaning hinges on Bertha's hidden identity as Rochester's wife, which the 'detective' Jane must expose.

Jane acts out the narrative of 'detection' until Bertha's identity is finally revealed. The reader is given a number of 'clues' as to her identity, and Rochester's attempts to cover up Bertha's existence become increasingly implausible as the novel progresses. Jane, in a sense, is a detective who must solve the 'crime' of Rochester's past life. Bertha's existence at Thornfield is evidence of Rochester's dishonesty.

Rochester, too, plays at being the detective. During his performance as a fortune-teller, he uses disguise to extract private information from Jane. (And Jane, in turn, must play the detective to see through Rochester's disguise). By obtaining 'proof' of her love for him, Rochester is able to plot his advance. Conversely, Jane tries in vain to detect signs of Rochester's love for her.

St John Rivers is a third detective in *Jane Eyre*. In his quest to unravel the mystery of Jane's origins, he collects evidence – her signature on the painting – and solves the mystery of her heritage. The 'mysteries' contained in these three narratives of detection – Jane and Rochester's love story, Bertha's true identity, and Jane's inheritance – effectively propel the narrative.

### Revenge plot

*Jane Eyre* can be seen to contain two separate narrative strands: a 'surface narrative' and a 'hidden narrative'. The surface narrative is a conventional story of a girl's progress as she grows into a woman, as discussed in the *Bildungsroman* section.

Yet an alternative reading is possible. While Jane appears to be innocent, it is hard not to notice that her foes often come to tragic ends. People who have wronged Jane come to grief with suspicious regularity.

If Jane is such a polite, honest and pleasant character, how does such an unobtrusive person get what she wants in her life so effectively? While Jane innocently goes about her business, it often seems as if a darker force is 'pulling the strings' for her.

Those who cross Jane's path tend to be punished in unusual ways. Further, these punishments are administered *in direct proportion* to their sins against Jane. Characters that have brutalised Jane are punished severely; characters that have merely inconvenienced her are punished mildly. The two characters who have wronged Jane most gravely – Mrs Reed and her son – are killed off. Mr Brocklehurst, who has humiliated Jane, loses his reputation. Bertha, who obstructs Jane's wish to marry Rochester, dies in Thornfield's conflagration. St John, who nearly derails Jane's life, is close to death at the novel's conclusion. And Rochester, who mistreats Jane yet still loves her, is severely injured.

The book's plot, then, punishes Jane's enemies in direct proportion to their acts. Notice, however, that Jane does not directly cause any of the injuries and deaths listed above – the plot does the work for her. This is essential, because Jane must always remain a sympathetic character. This 'revenge plot', in other words, enables Jane to remain the underdog even as her enemies are vanquished, because she never gets blood on her hands.

## Language

### Evocative and emotive language

The narrator uses language in evocative and unconventional ways. While many nineteenth-Century novels employed restrained prose, Jane's expression intensifies the emotional impact of her experiences.

Consider the following description of Jane's temptation to submit to Rochester:

> The whole consciousness of my life lorn, my love lost, my hope quenched, my faith death-struck swayed full and mighty above me in one sullen mass. That bitter hour cannot be described in truth, 'the waters came into my soul; I sank in deep mire: I felt no standing; I came into deep waters; the floods overflowed me. (p.342)

Jane's vivid metaphorical association of seduction with drowning allows the reader to 'feel' her mental state far more vividly; *Jane Eyre* contains many other instances of visual imagery being used to intensify emotional description.

## Psychological realism (i.e. natural description and the sublime)

While the landscape in *Jane Eyre* is realistically described, the natural world also seems to be responsive to Jane's desires. For example, when Jane is thinking about her forthcoming marriage, she has the following dream:

> ... the moon appeared momentarily in that part of the sky which filled their fissure; her disk was blood-red and half overcast; she seemed to throw on me one bewildered, dreary glance, and buried herself again instantly in the deep drift of cloud. (p.319)

While this is a realistic description of nature, it also beautifully conveys Jane's mounting anxiety about her upcoming marriage. Nature is presented in Brontë's work as a visual reflection of character's inner moods and feelings, and Jane often receives advice from the spirit of 'mother nature'. When considering Rochester's proposal, for example, this voice of nature commands her: 'My daughter, flee temptation'. Jane responds, 'Mother, I will' (p.367). While the novel's physical environment can therefore be considered 'objective' on one level, on another level it is also imbued with Jane's own desires.

## Childhood and adulthood perspectives

Brontë is particularly adept at using limited perspective, skilfully deploying the 'voice of childhood' in her work. The tension between the two voices is interesting, as the elder Jane looks back and reflects on her earlier life. As we all know, we become better at seeing situations in a wider perspective when we become older. As children, though, we often see things in a state of pure sensation.

When the young Jane is in the Red-Room, she intimates that 'ear, eye and mind were alike strained by dread, such dread as only children can feel' (p.24). On one level, Jane's childhood self interprets sensations virtually unmediated. They come at her in a rush, without the adult consciousness to filter and explain them. Yet on another, there are actually two narrative perspectives: the young child who is doing the experiencing, and the adult who is putting it in context for the reader. For example, here is Jane's description of her feelings after her confrontation with Mrs Reed:

> A child cannot quarrel with its elders, as I had done – cannot give its furious feelings uncontrolled play, as I had given mine – without experiencing afterwards the pang of remorse and the chill of reaction. (p.45)

The narrating Jane is able to make sense of the child's feelings; however, the younger Jane can only feel fear, without understanding why this happens. The difference in knowledge between the two Janes creates a sense of pity for the child, who is not in possession of the adult's more developed level of knowledge.

The gap between these two perspectives shrinks as the character's age approaches the narrator's; it finally vanishes completely. As readers, though, we benefit greatly from the book's dual perspective, because the more mature Jane is able to look back and try to make sense of some of her life's earlier events.

### Past and present tense

*Jane Eyre*'s narrator occasionally moves into the present tense, which provides the reader with an intense feeling of 'being there'. See, for example, the following scene:

> Two days are passed. It is a summer evening; the coachman has set me down at a place called Whitcross ... Whitcross is no town, nor even a hamlet; it is but a stone pillar set up where four roads meet ... From the well-known names of these towns I learn in what county I have lighted; a north-midland shire, dusk with moorland, ridged with mountain: this I see. (p.371)

The use of the present tense represents a mood of 'pure sensation', enabling Jane to convey her emotions to the reader with far greater immediacy than would be possible with a conventional narrative voice in the past tense.

# CHAPTER-BY-CHAPTER ANALYSIS

## Chapter I – Jane's mistreatment

### Key quote

'What does Bessie say I have done?' (p.9)

We first meet the orphan Jane when she is living with her aunt, Mrs Reed, and her cousins, John, Eliza and Georgiana.

Jane's story begins as a portrait of suffering. She is shown reading to escape her unhappy life, where her only solace is being able to escape into her own imagination with books. John Reed resents this, and physically abuses Jane when he finds her. After Jane retaliates, her aunt punishes her by sending her to the 'red-room' – solitary confinement in a room that Jane hates.

## Chapter II – Jane in the red-room

### Key quote

'Am I a servant?' (p.15)

The terrifying red-room in which Jane is incarcerated is laden with the imposing furniture of Jane's uncle, Mrs Reed's dead husband. Fuming against this injustice, Jane is finally released after she has an intense panic attack. Overcome with emotion after her release, Jane notes that 'unconsciousness closed the scene' (p.22).

### Key point

Although it takes place very early in Jane's life, the 'red-room' is perhaps the book's most vivid scene.

## Chapter III – Recovery

### Key quote

'For me, the watches of that long night passed in ghastly wakefulness...' (p.24)

Recovering from the red-room ordeal, Jane is nursed back to health by the kindly Bessie Leaven. To escape further ordeals at Gateshead, Jane agrees to go to Lowood boarding school.

20    Insight Study Guide

# Chapter IV – Another rebellion

**Key quote**

'My Uncle Reed is in heaven, and can see all you do and think; and so can papa and mamma: they know how you shut me up all day long, and how you wish me dead.' (p.34)

More miserable months pass at Gateshead. The friendless Jane's only comfort is her doll, because 'human beings must love something' (p.35). One day, Mr Brocklehurst arrives at Gateshead to assess Jane's suitability for Lowood. Although intimidated by him, she decides that Lowood cannot be as bad as her current life: after calling Mrs Reed 'hard-hearted' (p.44), Jane is sent to boarding school immediately. Mrs Reed tells Mr Brocklehurst that Jane has a bad character. After learning of her newfound freedom, Jane says: 'Even for me life had its gleams of sunshine' (p.48).

# Chapter V – Jane's first day at boarding school

**Key quote**

'As yet I had spoken to no one, nor did anybody seem to take notice of me; I stood lonely enough: but to that feeling of isolation I was accustomed; it did not oppress me much.' (p.58)

Jane hopes that Lowood will liberate her from her misery, only to find it even worse than Gateshead. The mistreated students are fed a nauseous mess of 'burnt porridge' (p.55), but to Jane's relief, a kindly teacher named Miss Temple provides the starving students with 'a lunch of bread and cheese' (p.57).

The school's austere 'church-like aspect' (p.58) makes the students fearful and obedient. But Jane's life improves somewhat when she meets the wise Helen Burns, to whom she immediately takes a liking.

# Chapter VI – Jane and Helen talk

**Key quote**

'You dirty, disagreeable girl! You have never cleaned your nails this morning!' (p.64)

Jane witnesses her new friend Helen being bullied by the sadistic Miss Scatcherd for not having cleaned her nails, even though the frozen water in the washbasin prevented her from doing so. Lacking Jane's rebellious spirit, Helen passively accepts others' savage criticisms of her, telling Jane that 'I live in calm, looking to the end' (p.70) in the true Christian tradition. Jane soon realises that she cannot accept such a life of self-denial.

## Chapter VII – Brocklehurst returns

### Key quote

'Miss Temple, Miss Temple, what – *what* is that girl with curled hair? Red hair, ma'am, curled – curled all over?' (p.75)

Brocklehurst's return to Lowood signals the most traumatic episode in Jane's schooling. He is a deeply misogynistic man (i.e. hostile to women), and seems to enjoy traumatising the students. The brutal and dehumanising scene in which Brocklehurst orders the girls' hair to be shaved off is almost unbearable – yet the unjust punishment is borne by each terrified and obedient girl without comment. Brocklehurst deliberately ruins Jane's fragile reputation at the school by repeating Mrs Reed's accusations against her.

After Jane is accused of breaking her slate, she is again punished severely. Yet even after being placed on a stool and branded a 'little castaway' (p.78), the resilient Jane takes comfort from a brave girl who dares to smile at her. (p.80)

### Key point

This is the most intense of the Lowood chapters, as it fully reveals the perverse attitude taken toward the children at the school.

## Chapter VIII – Jane and Helen dine with Miss Temple

### Key quote

'Mr Brocklehurst is not a god: nor is he even a great and admired man: he is little liked here...' (p.82)

When Jane and Helen are comforting each other, Miss Temple offers to clear Jane's name. The blissful time spent with Miss Temple is among Jane's happiest experiences.

In Miss Temple's quarters, the teacher shares her modest rations with Jane and Helen. The famished Jane remarks that 'we feasted that night as on nectar and ambrosia' (p.86). Helen seems utterly transformed by the experience. After learning of Miss Temple's generous efforts to clear her name, Jane joyfully observes: 'I would not now have exchanged Lowood with all its privations, for Gateshead and its daily luxuries' (p.89). In this chapter we learn that Helen is fatally ill.

## Chapter IX – Springtime and typhoid at Lowood

### Key quote

'That forest-dell, where Lowood lay, was the cradle of fog and fog-bred pestilence...' (p.91)

While springtime is usually seen as a season of renewal, spring at Lowood is marred by a typhus epidemic that kills off many of its vulnerable students.

While this event is undeniably a tragedy, Jane takes a curiously ambiguous attitude towards it. While acknowledging that the loss of life is a disaster, she also observes that it has a beneficial effect on the appallingly-run school, which becomes a far more pleasant place after the disease has swept through.

This relief is overshadowed by Helen's death, who expires believing that she will 'be received by the ... mighty universal Parent' (97). On hearing this, Jane realises that she lacks Helen's devout faith in a benevolent God. In a touching scene, Jane climbs into the dying Helen's bed and is found there in the morning, holding onto Helen's corpse in her sleep. At the end of this chapter, we learn that Jane is now ten years old.

## Chapter X – Jane leaves Lowood

### Key quote

'... grant me at least a new servitude!' (p.102)

Eight years pass. After Helen's untimely death, Jane no longer feels comfortable staying within the confines of Lowood. Her prayers to escape her bondage are granted when her attempt to find employment as a governess succeeds. After briefly encountering her childhood maid

Bessie, who is now married with a young son, Jane hopes that her own life will markedly improve as well.

Jane views her departure from Lowood virtually as an escape from prison. Shortly before securing the governess position, the desperate protagonist confesses that she 'walked around [her] chamber most of the time' (p.101). After gaining employment, her mood lifts: she looks forward with some trepidation to 'a new life in the unknown environs of Millcote' (p.110), her new employer's address.

## Key point

This chapter is one of the novel's 'turning points', as it significantly extends the physical boundaries of Jane's world.

## Chapter XI – Jane enters Thornfield

### Key quote

'A new chapter in a novel is something like a new scene in a play...' (p.111)

This chapter begins in an unusually optimistic mood. Jane's new employer Mrs Fairfax seems relatively kind; and her pupil, the coquettish (vain) French girl Adele, is well-behaved, though somewhat mischievous. After enduring the difficult life of the first ten chapters, Thornfield indeed seems to promise a new beginning.

But after Mrs Fairfax informs Jane of her responsibilities, two mysteries remain. Firstly, the mansion's owner, Mr Rochester, has not yet appeared. And secondly, Jane is puzzled as to the identity of the mysterious person who occasionally emits a 'curious laugh' from somewhere upstairs in the mansion (p.126). Although Mrs Fairfax assures Jane that the culprit is only Grace Poole, one of Thornfield's servants, Jane is not completely convinced.

## Chapter XII – Jane explores Thornfield

### Key quote

'It is in vain to say human beings ought to be satisfied with tranquillity: they must have action; and they will make it if they cannot find it.' (p.129)

Jane spends October and November fulfilling her duties as Adele's governess. She often hears the 'eccentric murmurs' of 'Grace Poole' (p.130), and wonders about her mental state. While exploring a nearby lane, Jane comes across a stranger who has fallen from his horse; she helps him back up and sends him and his dog, Pilot, on their way. Instead of politely introducing himself, the man abruptly questions Jane about her master's identity; she cannot answer him, however, as she has not yet met Rochester. After he has gone, Jane returns to the 'stagnation' of Thornfield (p.137), which is already beginning to affect her mood. Seeing the man's dog back at the house, Jane realises that the stranger is in fact Thornfield's owner, Mr Rochester.

## Chapter XIII – Meeting Rochester

### Key quote

'I knew my traveller, with his broad and jetty eyebrows, his square forehead, made squarer by the horizontal sweep of his black hair.' (p.141)

Jane does not have the opportunity to meet Rochester immediately, as he is exhausted from his journey. However, she is invited to have tea with Rochester and Adele at six o'clock the next day.

Jane's second meeting with Rochester does not go well at first. He initially seems quite like Brocklehurst: an aloof, dominating man who talked 'as a statue would' (p.142). However, Rochester's gruffness conceals a sense of humour. At times he seems to be gently mocking Jane, as when he jovially warns her not to 'fall back on over-modesty' (p.143).

As Rochester quizzes Jane about her past and compliments her paintings, he appears to be compiling information about her. Jane still does not take to him, though, finding him too 'changeful and abrupt' (p.149).

### Key point

Jane is properly introduced to the man who will eventually become her husband. From the beginning, the connection between them is evident.

## Chapter XIV – Rochester's confessions

### Key quote

'You examine me, Miss Eyre,' said he: 'do you think me handsome?' (p.154)

Upon meeting Rochester again, Jane finds herself becoming increasingly fascinated with him. Rochester is obviously in a better mood on this occasion, and questions Jane further about many aspects of her life. He also reveals some of the details about his past during their conversation, hinting of his sordid 'past existence' and calling himself a 'trite, commonplace sinner' (p.159). After Rochester admits his addiction to sexual pleasure, Jane warns him that 'it will taste bitter' (p.160) if not exercised within the bounds of marriage. Rochester seems grateful for Jane's advice, and the meeting ends on a positive note, with Rochester apparently improved by the experience.

## Chapter XV – Rochester's past

### Key quote

'You never felt jealously, did you, Miss Eyre? Of course not: I need not ask you: because you never felt love.' (p.166)

Rochester further elaborates on his dark and enigmatic past. For instance, he reveals that Adele is the 'illegitimate offspring of a French opera-girl' (p.170) – a term which often carried connotations of sexual immorality. He also talks of his decision to raise Adele in England. Even after these revelations, Jane confesses that she finds Rochester's face 'more cheering than the brightest fire' (p.172). However, her upbeat mood is cut short by the return of the 'demoniac laugh' (p.173) followed by a bizarre attempt on Rochester's life: Jane, realising that someone has tried to burn him to death in his bed, saves his life by dragging him from the flames.

Recovering from the attack, Rochester convinces Jane that the mysterious Grace Poole is to blame. He also tells Jane that he is forever in her debt (p.176).

## Chapter XVI – Rochester's departure

### Key quote

'I wanted to hear his voice again, yet feared to meet his eye.' (p.178)

While Jane ponders why Grace Poole would attempt to kill Rochester, Rochester himself temporarily departs Thornfield. Anxiously awaiting his return, Jane discovers that several rich socialites have arrived at the house – one of whom is Blanche Ingram, apparently Rochester's love interest.

Angrily calling herself 'Poor stupid dupe' (p.186), Jane resigns herself to the fact that Rochester never really loved her after all. In an attempt to overcome her obsession with Rochester, Jane makes a sketch of the beautiful Blanche Ingram in her room.

## Chapter XVII – Rochester's return

**Key quote**

'I know I must conceal my sentiments; I must smother hope; I must remember that he cannot care much for me.' (p.204)

When Rochester returns to Thornfield, Jane compares herself unfavourably to the attractive and glamorous guests. Yet she notices, with satisfaction, the shallowness and vapidity of this privileged crowd. Blanche is clearly angling to secure a proposal of marriage from Rochester, who appears to treat her with indifference.

## Chapter XVIII – The game of charades

**Key quote**

'I have told you, reader, that I had learnt to love Mr Rochester; I could not unlove him now, merely because I found that he had ceased to notice me...' (p.215)

Having witnessed Blanche's inept attempts to tempt Rochester, Jane soon develops a sense of contempt towards her, triumphantly observing that *'she could not charm him'* (p.216). Jane is slowly gaining confidence in her own personal qualities.

The charades and celebrations are interrupted by the unexpected arrival of a man named Mason, followed by a grizzled fortune-teller who offers to tell the fortunes of those in attendance. The guests enthusiastically jump at the chance.

## Chapter XIX – Fortune-telling

**Key quote**

'Can I help you, sir? – I'd give my life to serve you.' (p.236)

Summoning Jane into the parlour, the fortune-teller subjects her to a strange series of puzzles and riddles. She mysteriously appears to know all about Jane's love for Rochester, among much other personal information about her. After drawing Jane into a long and revealing conversation, the fortune-teller reveals 'herself' as Rochester in disguise. Jane strongly disapproves of this trick: as she scolds, 'it was not right' (p.234).

Rochester becomes distressed when he learns that Mason is at the house, and asks Jane to spy on the newcomer for him. He soon recovers from the initial shock, and returns to his old self.

## Key point

Although Rochester is disguised at this point, it is now clear that he is going to great lengths to win Jane over.

## Chapter XX – An attack on Mason

### Key quote

'To live for me, Jane, is to stand on a crater-crust which may crack and spue fire any day.' (p.250)

Jane and Rochester wake to the sound of Mason being attacked – presumably by Grace Poole. Nursing him back to health on Rochester's orders, Jane becomes increasingly convinced that Grace is not the evil presence in the house.

The injured Mason departs after being bandaged, and Rochester taunts Jane about his impending marriage to Blanche – Jane bears this teasing with quiet dignity.

## Chapter XXI – The deaths of John and Mrs Reed

### Key quotes

'Feeling without judgement is a washy draft indeed; but judgement untempered by feeling is too bitter and husky a morsel for human deglutition.' (p.272)

'I could not forget your conduct to me, Jane – the fury with which you once turned on me ...' (p.275)

Jane learns of John Reed's suicide and Mrs Reed's consequent stroke. Mrs Reed, after hearing of her son's death, calls for Jane, who departs from Thornfield to meet her. As Jane leaves, she tells Rochester that she knows of his plan to marry Blanche, and suggests that he put Adele into care.

Returning to Gateshead, Jane is reunited with Georgiana and Eliza, the cousins with whom she grew up. During her stay at Gateshead, she witnesses the two sisters' bitter mutual animosity.

At her aunt's deathbed, Jane learns of her mysterious uncle's wish to adopt her as a daughter – news which her aunt had previously concealed from her. Recalling Jane's childhood insubordination, her ailing aunt angrily tells Jane that she 'was born ... to be [her] torment' (p.275). Mrs Reed dies without reconciling with Jane.

## Key point

Two of Jane's major enemies are despatched in quick succession. This can be seen as the beginning of her real turn of fortune.

## Chapter XXII – Jane returns to Thornfield

### Key quote

'I was going back to Thornfield: but how long was I to stay there? Not long; of that I was sure.' (p.280)

Jane returns to Rochester, keen to see him again although she knows he is now 'taken'. Rochester is undergoing wedding preparations, but Jane notes with some hope that he has not visited his bride-to-be, and admits to the reader that she had 'never ... loved him so well' (p.285).

## Chapter XXIII – Rochester proposes

### Key quote

'I have known you, Mr Rochester, and it strikes me with terror and anguish to feel I absolutely must be torn from you forever. I see the necessity of departure; and it is like looking at the necessity of death.' (p.292)

Meeting Jane in the grounds of Thornfield, Rochester tells her that she must find a new position, offering to help establish her as a teacher in Ireland. The distraught Jane heavily hints at her true feelings for Rochester, and he promises to spend time with her shortly before she leaves.

Rochester then cryptically declares his love for Jane, and she reciprocates by openly declaring her love for him. Rochester then reveals that Blanche was a decoy: he had intended to marry Jane all along. The stunned Jane accepts his proposal, and the two finally embrace.

## Key point

Many of Jane's misconceptions about Rochester are resolved in this chapter, and the barriers between them seem to finally have broken down. Unfortunately, this is not the case.

## Chapter XXIV – Jane and Rochester's courtship

### Key quote

'While arranging my hair, I looked at my face in the glass, and felt it was no longer plain...' (p.297)

Jane's life has changed dramatically in a very short time. She is now openly in love with Rochester, and eagerly anticipates being 'caressed by him' (p.298). He excites her with talk of their wedding, and Jane becomes intoxicated with extravagant future plans. Rochester and Jane flirt and banter in this happy chapter, which is perhaps the novel's most conventionally romantic. The tactless Mrs Fairfax cannot comprehend Rochester's attraction to Jane, and warns her that he may be trying to seduce her without marrying her. Adele, however, seems to approve of the match.

Rochester's wedding preparations begin to irritate Jane, who fears that he is trying to turn her into another version of Blanche. She refuses his offer to buy her exotic clothing, stating her preference for far more modest attire. Jane warns Rochester that she will not be his 'ape in a harlequin's jacket' (p.299), and demands to be treated as an equal in marriage. She also privately worries that she is becoming overly obsessed with her future husband.

## Chapter XXV – Jane's wedding preparations

### Key quote

'I wish he would come! I wish he would come!' I exclaimed, seized with hypochondriac foreboding.' (p.320)

Rochester leaves Thornfield, and Jane becomes increasingly anxious about his absence. When they joyfully reunite, he informs her of his plans to take Jane away from Thornfield after their marriage. Although they are clearly looking forward to the marriage with great anticipation, Jane confesses that she has been having nightmares about 'some barrier dividing us' (p.324). To Rochester, she relates a disturbingly vivid 'dream' of a hideous figure who loomed over her in her sleep and ripped her veil in half. As before, Rochester insists that the woman must have been Grace Poole.

# Chapter XXVI – The wedding

### Key quote

'The marriage cannot go on: I declare the existence of an impediment.' (p.333)

The wedding begins according to plan, although Jane notices two strangers in attendance. Halfway through the ceremony, one of the strangers announces that the marriage cannot go ahead.

A solicitor named Briggs dramatically reveals that Rochester has a wife still living. The other stranger is Mason, who turns out to be Rochester's current wife's brother. Rochester defiantly admits that he is indeed already married, and reveals his current wife as the mad woman who haunts Thornfield. He introduces the guests to this depraved figure, named Bertha, whom Jane recognises as the monster from her 'dream'. Jane, realising that Rochester was planning to commit bigamy, ends the chapter in a state of utter despair.

## Key point

The events of this chapter separate Jane Eyre from a conventional love story. Jane's troubles are just beginning.

# Chapter XXVII – The aftermath

### Key quote

'Jane, I never meant to wound you thus.' (p.344)

Rochester attempts to apologise to Jane and justify his actions. Despite his protestations, however, Jane resolves to leave Thornfield immediately. Drawing on her vast inner reserves of strength, she resists his pleas to keep her as his mistress. In a desperate attempt to prevent Jane from fleeing, Rochester reveals further details of his life story – including how he was deceived in the West Indies by his wife's family into marrying the 'intemperate and unchaste' Bertha (p.353), and his contemplation of suicide afterwards. He describes Bertha's descent into total insanity and the necessity of locking her up in the attic at Thornfield. In a heart-wrenching scene, Jane, fearing that she will simply become one more in a long line of Rochester's mistresses, resolves to leave Thornfield forever.

## Key point

Rochester is deluded about the impact of his wife's existence, and tries to convince Jane that they can stay together. But it is already too late.

# Chapter XXVIII – Arrival at Moor House

**Key quote**

'My rest might have been blissful enough, only a sad heart broke it.' (p.373)

After leaving Thornfield by coach, the starving and destitute Jane finds herself in the locality of Whitcross, where she sinks into sleep. Stumbling exhaustedly towards the lights of a house, Jane is taken inside by two kindly women: Mary and Diana Rivers. After their brother arrives, Jane is sent to bed.

# Chapter XXIX – Meeting St John Rivers

**Key quote**

'Not a tie links me to any living thing: not a claim do I possess to admittance under any roof in England.' (p.397)

Jane's hosts make her welcome, and she learns that her new residence is Moor House in the town of Marsh End. The servant, Hannah, is outwardly rough but fundamentally kind; and St John's sisters are friendly and compassionate. St John himself, though, is an intense, imposing figure with 'an Athenian mouth and chin' (p.396), and a manner resembling Brocklehurst's. When questioned about her past, Jane takes on the alias 'Jane Elliott' to protect her identity, as she knows Rochester will be seeking her.

# Chapter XXX – Jane's friendship with Mary and Diana develops

**Key quote**

'St John looks quiet, Jane; but he hides a fever in his vitals.' (p.410)

Jane's friendship with the Rivers sisters blossoms, but her relationship with St John remains prickly. She sees him as a distant, remote and imposing figure, and is acutely aware of the painful contrast with her beloved Rochester.

But St John soon reveals his caring side by offering Jane a position at a village school, which she gladly accepts. When the Rivers learn of their uncle's death, Jane is surprised at their lack of mourning for the deceased. Jane soon leaves Marsh End for her new position in Morton.

## Chapter XXXI – Jane's new position

**Key quote**

'Much enjoyment I do not expect in the life opening before me: yet it will, doubtless, if I regulate my mind, and exert my powers as I ought, yield me enough to live on from day to day.' (p.413)

Jane begins her new job in Morton with thoughts of Rochester foremost in her mind. Yet while she misses him, she is glad that she has 'adhered to principle' rather than sinking 'in the silken snare' of adultery (p.414). Although finding her new job difficult, Jane welcomes its fortifying effects on her spirit.

Afterwards, St John tells Jane the story of his life, including how becoming a missionary saved him from despair. Inspired, Jane resolves to become a missionary too. Their conversation is interrupted by the arrival of Miss Rosamond Oliver – a woman whom St John strongly desires, yet whose puritanical religious beliefs will not permit him to love.

## Chapter XXXII – St John's passion

**Key quote**

'...I would far rather be where I am than in any high family in the land.' (p.426)

Jane grows into her teaching position, even beginning to enjoy it a little. Rosamond visits her regularly, and the two become friends despite their clear differences. Jane sketches Rosamond, and is very pleased with the likeness. Her creativity and happiness are re-emerging in this new environment.

St John finally 'opens up' about his true feelings for Rosamond after seeing Jane's painting. Yet he also reveals his loathing for this intense attraction: 'Reason, and not feeling, is my guide', he tells her (p.432). Jane begins to comprehend how cold St John actually is, and realises he will never marry Rosamond.

## Chapter XXXIII – St John visits Jane

**Key quote**

'It seemed I had found a brother ...' (p.444)

After discovering Jane's true identity from the signature on her painting, St John reveals his knowledge of her entire life story, including her aborted marriage to Rochester. He then announces that Jane has inherited a fortune of twenty thousand pounds from her recently-deceased uncle, and tells Jane that he and his sisters are her cousins. When the delighted Jane realises that her hosts are family, she resolves to share her fortune with them equally.

## Chapter XXXIV – St John's proposal

**Key quote**

'I scorn your idea of love.' (p.471)

Christmas with her newfound family represents another idyllic period of Jane's life. However, Jane finds St John difficult to be around as he seems increasingly interested in her, but always remains very cold. St John asks Jane to come to India with him as his wife and fellow-missionary, which she agrees to – on the condition that they go as fellow-missionaries rather than as husband and wife. When he refuses and insists they must marry, Jane changes her mind after a terrible struggle with St John's overwhelming personality.

### Key point

This is Jane's next major test of strength. It takes immense willpower to reject St John's offer of marriage.

## Chapter XXXV – Jane's decision

**Key quote**

'God did not give me my life to throw away.' (p.477)

St John delays his departure in order to remind Jane of the consequences of her decision, calling her scornful rejection of his offer of marriage 'violent, unfeminine, and untrue' (p.475). Jane replies that she is 'not under the slightest obligation' to go to India with him as 'a fitting fellow-labourer in his Indian toils' (p.477–78). However, Jane's resolve soon crumbles under pressure, and she almost agrees to marry St John – until she hears Rochester's desperate voice summon her from afar. This aural vision gives her the courage to make a decisive break from St John, and she leaves for Thornfield the following morning.

## Chapter XXXVI – Jane's return to Thornfield

### Key quote

'I looked with timorous joy towards a stately house: I saw a blackened ruin.' (p.489)

Jane arrives at Thornfield, only to find it destroyed. According to an innkeeper, Rochester was made 'blind and a cripple' by the fire, and Bertha is 'as dead as the stones on which her brains and blood were scattered' (p.494). Concluding that Rochester has now been freed from his marital ties, Jane learns of his existence as a recluse in Ferndean, a secluded place around thirty miles from Thornfield.

## Chapter XXXVII – Jane and Rochester reunited

### Key quote

'My dear master', I answered, 'I am Jane Eyre: I have found you out – I am come back to you.' (p.500)

Jane goes to Ferndean to surprise the now-blind Rochester, and they are finally reunited. Rochester is crippled and emasculated, but the love between the two remains as strong as ever. Rochester jealously quizzes Jane about her feelings for St John, and she promises Rochester that her love for him remains. Rochester also reveals that he spoke the words she heard on the previous night, creating a profound link which reinforces their spiritual bond.

# Chapter XXXVIII – Jane and Rochester's marriage

## Key quote

'Reader, I married him.' (p.517)

Jane and Rochester's wedding is the opposite of the original: a humble affair without pretence or ostentation. This chapter spans ten years of Jane's married life, during which she and Rochester have a child together. Rochester gradually regains his sight, and the novel closes with the news of St John's impending death in India.

## Key point

Jane is finally rewarded for her strength under adversity in this chapter, where she is finally able to experience love with Rochester on her own terms.

# CHARACTERS & RELATIONSHIPS

## Jane Eyre

### Key quote

'The more solitary, the more friendless, the more unsustained I am, the more I will respect myself.' (p.365)

Jane seems to embody a paradox. She is plain and demure on one level, yet determined to succeed at all costs on another. Her secret is her unbreakable will – an inner fire that burns after others' have been exhausted.

Over the course of her story, Jane undergoes many hardships. Why, then, is this such an uplifting novel?

*Jane Eyre* is a far more optimistic book than it might seem, because Jane's will can never be crushed. Her ferocious desire to flourish in her life of limited opportunities is the exact opposite of Helen Burns' love of passivity and death, or of St John's perverse emphasis on self-denial in the face of God's love. Jane will have none of this: for her, life is an opportunity for self-expression, not a dreary waiting-room that one must stay in before going to heaven.

Although Jane rejects religious self-denial, she doesn't indulge in indiscriminate earthly pleasures. Jane is a finely-balanced character: charting a firm course between a stifling life of self-denial and a dissolute life of sensual pleasure, her path towards true happiness and fulfilment is always precarious. Unafraid to make difficult and painful choices for the sake of maintaining her own integrity, Jane negotiates the challenges that she encounters with true courage.

That is not to say that she isn't tempted. Jane almost falls into the trap of assenting to powerful people: the first time when she almost agrees to live 'in sin' with Rochester; the second when she almost agrees to accompany St John to India. One is a potential crime of passion, the other a crime of self-denial. Yet Jane retains great confidence in the merits of her own choices throughout, and does not fall into the trap of letting others determine the course of her life. Although her final destination at Ferndean is humble, Jane can rest content in the knowledge that she remained true to her principles. Her twin ambitions – to find friendship and love – have been fulfilled.

# Love interests

Jane is courted by two men, for very different reasons and with very different results. The pair can be seen to form opposite sides of the human character, and again represent twin challenges for Jane to negotiate.

## Jane and Rochester

### Key quotes

'Mr Rochester, I must leave you.'

'For how long, Jane? For a few minutes, while you smooth your hair ...?' (p.350)

Jane and Rochester are extraordinarily passionate characters who are evenly matched. The story of their developing love is one of gradually overcoming the apparently insuperable obstacles that have been thrown in their path.

At first, the romance seems as if it will not work because of the conflicting personalities of the two characters. Rochester is a tall, imposing figure, similar to Brocklehurst in many ways – bent on dominating all the women in his life, he initially overpowers the demure, obedient governess.

But Jane's inexplicable power gradually makes Rochester lose hold of his dominant position over her. His dependence on Jane robs him of his masculine power, and places him in a subservient position that he is unused to. (Jane's commanding acts of getting Rochester back onto his horse, rescuing him from a fire, and tending for him when he is incapacitated suggest that she, not he, is the dominant force in their relationship at these times.)

Their wedding ceremony is interrupted by the revelation of Rochester's previous marriage to the grotesque invalid Bertha, who haunts the upper floor of Thornfield. In this, Rochester's lowest moment, Jane finally rejects him.

It takes an extraordinary event to make Rochester Jane's equal. In the closing chapter, the crippled Rochester finally loses his threatening air of masculinity.

### Jane and St John

'I scorn the counterfeit sentiment you offer: yes, St John, and I scorn you when you offer it.' (p.471)

After fleeing Thornfield, Jane meets the imperious (dominating) St John at Millcote. St John (pronounced 'Sin-Jun') initially comes across as extremely well-suited to Jane's personality. Both are highly moralistic, with a desire to help others and a compassionate nature.

But St John is only superficially admirable. In fact, he is the novel's most aggressive example of dominating patriarchy, made all the more insidious because his aggression is cloaked in Christian charity. St John distorts his personality by repressing his feelings for the beautiful Rosamond, and forces himself to become a creature of pure reason.

Jane's rejection of St John's offer of marriage is her greatest triumph. He reacts to her refusal with scorn and fury. Yet Jane's rejection of St John's sterile offer opens a path to her reconciliation with Rochester.

St John, then, represents the 'rational' side of human feeling, while Rochester can be seen as the 'emotional' side. The ultimate victory in *Jane Eyre* is the protagonist's transcendence of the concerns of the head for the more urgent concerns of the heart.

## Friends

Because the central love story is so compelling, it is easy to forget that *Jane Eyre* is just as much about friendship as it is about love. Jane's overwhelming desire for friendship is obvious from the first page, when she weeps on hearing Bessie sing 'God is a friend to the poor orphan child' (p.27). When longing for escape from Lowood, she sadly states that 'I have no friends' (p.102), and much later admits to Diana and Mary that she is 'absolutely without home and friends' (p.397). This isolation is a constant thorn in Jane's side. Although she habitually draws on her inner resources, her sense of loneliness is acute. Before eventually finding true friendship with her cousins at Moor House, Jane forms several friendships that are prematurely truncated.

## Jane and Helen Burns

**Key quote**

'I believe God is good; I can resign my immortal part to Him without any misgiving. God is my father; God is my friend: I love Him; I believe He loves me.' (p.97)

Helen, Jane's only friend at Lowood, can be seen as the idealised version of traditional femininity. As her surname suggests, Helen's goodness is consumed by her time at Lowood, where her will is devoured by the cruelty surrounding her. In this sense, Helen functions as a martyr-figure. After Helen's untimely death, Jane makes a point of visiting her grave.

Helen is also subjected to the routine humiliations that the students at Lowood have to endure. For example, after leaving her room untidy, Helen is forced to wear a sign with the word 'Slattern' (approximately the modern word 'slob', with an undertone of 'slut') affixed to her forehead (p.87). The injustice of this label makes Helen's patient bearing of her cruel punishment all the more admirable – yet Jane cannot relate to this extreme passivity.

## Jane and Miss Temple

**Key quote**

'...the breakfast was so ill-prepared that the pupils could not possibly eat it; and I dared not allow them to remain fasting until dinner-time.' (p.74)

As her name suggests, Miss Temple functions as a guiding light for Jane. Her acts of compassion toward the students are a source of solace for Jane during her eight long years at boarding school. Although Miss Temple is a deeply compassionate person, she is given few opportunities to care for others at Lowood.

One of the narrative's most poignant moments relates Miss Temple's act of mercy for the children after they are given burnt porridge. Bringing them some bread and cheese from her own supply, Miss Temple rejects the school's harsh disciplinary attitude and attempts to introduce something more humane.

Although she is more of a mother-figure than a friend to Jane, Miss Temple nevertheless provides Jane and Helen with pleasant conversation and a caring environment in a time when these things are otherwise absent.

### Diana and Mary

'Indeed you *shall* stay here.' (p.400)

Jane's cousins, whom she meets when on the edge of starvation, are a perfect fit for Jane's own personality. Highly educated and cultured, speaking multiple languages and familiar with great works of literature, they are mutually delighted with Jane's unexpected arrival into their lives. They are also compassionate, rescuing Jane from poverty and taking her into their house without resentment – far different to St John's bloodless Christian charity. Polar opposites to their icy brother, they make Jane's struggle with St John's personality easier by supporting her judgements: as Jane confides, 'Diana Rivers had designated her brother "inexorable as death". She had not exaggerated.' (p.421)

Jane's decision to donate three-quarters of her inheritance to the Rivers siblings binds the friends together most firmly. The decision represents the most natural thing in the world for Jane: 'I could not forego the delicious pleasure of which I have caught a glimpse – that of repaying, in part, a mighty obligation, and winning to myself life-long friends' (p.446).

Diana and Mary are quite similar to one another, and their small differences are overshadowed by the vast gulf between them and their brother. They are also perhaps too beneficent to be genuinely interesting characters, yet they at least give Jane the chance to achieve one of her major goals in life.

## Enemies and rivals

### Jane and Mrs Reed

'Children must be corrected for their faults.' (p.45)

In many ways, Mrs Reed perfectly fits the role of the 'evil stepmother', familiar to us from fairy tales. There is a clear similarity, for example, between Jane's confinement in the Red Room and Cinderella's (or even Harry Potter's) confinement under the stairs. All of these sympathetic childhood figures are abused by unpleasant step-parents.

But one element separates Mrs Reed from the typical stepmother-figure: dominance. In the traditional fairy tale, the dominating parent-figures are strong, while the children are weak. In *Jane Eyre*, however,

Mrs Reed is a particularly weak character. Although she has the power to physically confine Jane, she never recovers from Jane's full-blooded rebellion against her tyrannical behaviour.

Absolutely entrenched in her privileged position as a dominating aristocrat, Mrs Reed is not emotionally prepared for Jane's verbal assault. Her treatment of Jane is explicitly tied to class: Jane is made to feel like a burden because she cannot pay her way. Jane eventually takes her revenge, however. At Mrs Reed's funeral, Jane coldly notes that she had not 'dropped a tear' (p.277).

### Jane and Brocklehurst

## Key quote

'Oh madam, when you put bread and cheese, instead of burnt porridge, into these children's mouths, you may indeed feed their vile bodies, but you little think how you starve their immortal souls!' (p.75)

The worst of *Jane Eyre*'s misogynists, Brocklehurst embodies patriarchal oppression. Brocklehurst is a threatening male presence who savagely punishes women for their sexual natures.

Portrayed unsympathetically, Brocklehurst is vulnerable to becoming a parody of himself when seemingly at the height of his powers: the sympathy felt for him is inversely proportional to his looming physical presence.

Brocklehurst's dignity is destroyed when his criminal negligence is exposed. After disease rips through Jane's school, the public find out about the 'wretched clothing and accommodations', which 'produced a result mortifying to Mr Brocklehurst' (p.99).

Although Brocklehurst is superficially similar to Rochester, they differ in their attitude toward women. While Rochester is eventually able to develop a genuine sense of love for Jane, Rochester's fear of women's sexuality aligns him more closely with St John Rivers.

### Jane and Miss Scatcherd

## Key quote

'Such is the imperfect nature of man! Such spots are there on the disc of the clearest planet; and eyes like Miss Scatcherd's can only see those minute defects, and are blind to the full brightness of the orb.' (p.80)

Brocklehurst's female counterpart, Miss Scatcherd (a name that sounds suspiciously like 'scratch hard' or 'scratch her') is chiefly responsible for the mistreatment of the students. Jane's symbolic victory over Miss Scatcherd occurs when she throws Helen's humiliating 'Slattern' sign in the fire.

Although Miss Scatcherd's eventual fate is not stated, she presumably loses her job when the epidemic exposes the school as a cruel and abusive institution.

### Jane and Blanche Ingram

**Key quote**

'Whenever I marry ... I am resolved my husband shall not be a rival, but a foil to me.' (p.208)

Blanche Ingram is Jane's main rival for Rochester's hand, and Jane's opposite in many ways. It is interesting, though, to note the contrast between their personalities. While Blanche is assertive in her own way, she is entirely focused on improving her social position. Her obsession with appearances contrasts starkly with Jane's modesty. While Jane is intensely jealous of Blanche, the latter's self-obsession makes her ineligible for Rochester's love.

### Jane and Bertha

**Key quote**

'The maniac bellowed: she parted her shaggy locks from her visage, and gazed wildly at her visitors. I recognised that purple face – those bloated features.' (p.338)

In many ways, the relationship between Jane and Bertha is the most psychologically complex and interesting in the novel. Although they never exchange a word, their connection is much deeper than it at first seems.

The two characters' situations are similar in many ways. Both are dominated and exploited by strong men in their lives, and both are subjected to physical abuse and incarceration.

There are some even more striking similarities. For example, the 'patriarchal death-chamber' in which Jane is imprisoned at the novel's opening resembles Bertha's stifling attic at Thornfield (Gilbert & Gubar 1984, p.340). Both spaces represent male efforts to confine or imprison threatening women.

Bertha, then, can be interpreted as a kind of 'double' for Jane as well as an enemy; that is, she represents darker impulses that Jane cannot directly articulate. In this view, Bertha represents the dark and unacceptable aspects of Jane's personality. Jane combines a demure appearance with an impressive capacity for rage, while Bertha expresses pure rage without the benefits of this concealment.

Jane's and Bertha's life stories are similar in many ways. Both have lost their entire families – Jane by death, and Bertha by Rochester's marriage. Both are imprisoned – Jane in the Red Room, and Bertha in Thornfield. And both are prone to fits of rage, directed against those who have wronged them.

But there is another way in which Bertha shadows Jane: the actions that she performs can be seen as the things that Jane herself wants to do. For example, Bertha's attempt to burn Rochester in his bed can been interpreted as a way of expressing Jane's underlying hostility toward him for his attempts to dominate her.

Yet although Bertha seems like a part of Jane, this part of her cannot survive. The death of Bertha in the fire at the novel's conclusion can be seen as a kind of 'exorcism' of Jane's pent-up rage that she has unleashed on others throughout her life. After Bertha's death, Jane and Rochester are finally able to marry.

# THEMES, IDEAS & VALUES

## The 'social problem' novel

*Jane Eyre*'s elements of fantasy make it easy to overlook Brontë's efforts to expose society's injustices.

Charlotte Brontë's school life was quite similar to Jane's. She also attended a brutal boarding school, where two of her sisters died. In Brontë's time, children often lived in horrific conditions, particularly in institutions such as boarding schools and orphanages.

The 'social problem' novel represented an attempt on behalf of several nineteenth century novelists to expose society's cruelty. The most famous social problem novelist was Charles Dickens, whose *Nicholas Nickleby* covers similar territory to *Jane Eyre*. Compare the following descriptions of Jane and Nicholas' schooling experiences:

> [Brontë] Our clothing was insufficient to protect us from the severe cold ... the scanty supply of food was distressing ... whenever the famished great girls had an opportunity they would coax or menace the little ones out of their portion. (*Jane Eyre*, p.71)

Nicholas' experiences are similar:

> [Dickens] Poor Nicholas, in addition to bad food, dirty lodging, and the being compelled to witness one dull unvarying round of squalid misery, was treated with every special indignity that malice could suggest, or the most grasping cupidity put upon him. (*Nicholas Nickleby*, ch. 12)

These and similar novels played a role in the creation of child-protection laws. Yet the safeguards we take for granted today – including a ban on child labour and the legal protection of children within families – were often ferociously resisted by the wealthy in Victorian England.

## Masochism and repression

*Jane Eyre* links female oppression to masochism – that is, the desire to cause mental or physical self-harm. Helen Burns is destroyed by this emotion, uncritically taking on board others' unfair criticisms. For example, Helen falsely believes that 'I am, as Miss Scatcherd said, slatternly' (p.67).

Yet inside this browbeaten exterior lies a passionate individual:

> The refreshing meal, the brilliant fire, the presence and kindness of her beloved instructress, or, perhaps, more than all these, something in her own unique mind, had roused her powers within her. They woke, they kindled: first, they glowed in the bright tint of her cheek, which till this hour I had never seen but pale and bloodless ... (p.86)

Helen's resurgence is only temporary: after the supper ends, she retreats into self-hatred once again.

On at least one occasion, Jane lapses into a similarly masochistic mindset. When she discovers Rochester's engagement to Blanche, she angrily turns on herself:

> 'You', I said, 'a favourite with Mr Rochester? ... Poor stupid dupe! – Could not even self-interest make you wiser? You repeated to yourself this morning the brief scene of last night? – Cover your face and be ashamed!' (p.186)

Fortunately, Jane, unlike Helen, learns to trust her inner sense of self-worth and discard this toxic sense of self-loathing.

## 'True love' and Romanticism

Women in Brontë's day often married for reasons other than love. In particular, women were encouraged to make 'advantageous' marriages to rich men.

Jane expressed disdain for such mercenary concepts of love. Again, Blanche Ingram provides a contrast. While Blanche changes her mind about marrying Rochester when she hears that he does not possess a large fortune (a falsehood), Rochester's fortune means nothing to Jane.

Jane and Rochester's 'true love' is expressed through their connection with natural and supernatural forces. Two moments in particular reflect this bond. In the first, Rochester's proposal of marriage to Jane is immediately followed by a 'sign' from nature:

> The great horse-chestnut at the bottom of the orchard had been struck by lightning in the night, and half of it split away. (p.296)

The symbolic 'splitting' of the tree accurately predicts the couple's future separation. Similarly, a supernatural event informs Jane of the possibility of reconciliation with Rochester. After rejecting St John's demands, Jane is summoned from a distance:

> I heard a voice somewhere cry — 'Jane! Jane! Jane! – nothing more ... it was the voice of a human being – a known, loved, well-remembered voice – that of Edward Fairfax Rochester; and it spoke in pain and woe, wildly, eerily, urgently. (p.483)

Rochester had in fact been crying out to Jane at that very moment. By making the protagonists' love for one another a part of the supernatural world, Brontë suggests that their love for each other transcends the physical.

## Sexuality

While *Jane Eyre* is a heavily dramatic book, it is subtle in its representation of Jane's sexuality. Victorian censorship made it impossible to directly represent sex, but Brontë is also making a wider point. Despite her paleness, littleness, and quietness, Jane obviously feels passion:

> 'I have something in my brain and heart, in my blood and nerves, which assimilates me mentally to him.' (p.203)

Jane's sexuality is also revealed to be important during St John's offer of marriage, which she rejects rather than accepting a life devoid of sensuality:

> Can I receive from him the bridal ring, endure all the forms of love (which I doubt not he would scrupulously observe) and know that the spirit was quite absent? (p.467)

This is contrasted with the obvious sexual elements of Jane's interactions with Rochester. At Ferndean, Jane is finally made 'bone of his bone and flesh of his flesh' (p.519).

Jane's refusal to see physical desire as corrupt was unusual in a time when the 'purity' of Victorian women was highly valued. Women were often thought to lack sexual desire entirely – an idea which Jane's experience refutes.

## Feminism and injustice

Jane is distinguished by her rejection of patriarchy, as represented by the various men that she confronts and ultimately defeats. Her own values are shown to be either morally superior or stronger than her society's, and her assertive femininity is contrasted with other, deficient versions. Blanche represents the accepted passive feminine ideal, yet *Jane Eyre* scorns this dehumanising concept of female beauty.

Jane speaks in the language of human equality, demanding to be treated as equal to her more powerful adversaries.

> 'Do you think I am an automaton? – a machine without feelings? and can bear to have my morsel of bread snatched from my lips, and my drop of living water dashed from my cup? Do you think, because I am poor, obscure, plain, and little, I am soulless and heartless? You think wrong! – I have as much soul as you, – and full as much heart!' (p.292)

This resembles the Jewish moneylender Shylock's plea for empathy in Shakespeare's *The Merchant of Venice*:

> 'Hath not a Jew eyes? Hath not a Jew hands, organs, dimensions, senses, affections, passions; fed with the same food, hurt with the same weapons, subject to the same diseases, heal'd by the same means, warm'd and cool'd by the same winter and summer, as a Christian is? If you prick us, do we not bleed? If you tickle us, do we not laugh? If you poison us, do we not die? And if you wrong us, do we not revenge?' (3.1.58–68)

In both instances, a member of an oppressed minority – women and Jews respectively – are given complexity and dignity by their authors.

It is hard today to understand how radical Jane's viewpoints were in relation to her time. When Brontë was writing, women were still deemed to be the property of their husbands under English law, and the woman's property would automatically go to her husband after her death. Men were legally allowed to beat their wives – or even rape them, if they were denied sex within marriage. Rochester betrays these attitudes when he threatens rape (in very veiled terms): 'Jane! will you hear reason? ... because, if you won't, I'll try violence' (p.349). He later refrains from violating Jane only because he fears losing her love: 'If I tear, if I rend the slight prison, my outrage would only let the captive loose' (p.366). These attitudes, while extreme, reflect Rochester's position as a dominant member of his society.

# The fragmented self

Jane's ferocious and unpredictable emotional states challenge the stable vision of the self.

Novelistic characters are built up through their patterns of behaviour. We 'get to know' a fictional character when we are able to predict how they will react to certain situations, just as we gradually become better at judging how our friends will react.

Yet Jane's behaviour is often surprising and highly unpredictable. She has a tendency to 'project' her emotions:

> 'Unjust! – unjust!' said my reason, ... and Resolve, equally wrought up, instigated some strange expedient to achieve escape from insupportable oppression ... (p.19)

Often, however, Jane's inner voices conflict with one another: when she becomes aware of her attraction to Rochester, she worries that 'sense would resist delirium: judgement would warn passion' (p.177). By playing aspects of herself off against one another, Jane is able to negotiate her spiritual difficulties.

Rochester too thinks in this way:

> 'Go', said Hope, 'and live again in Europe: there it is not known what a sullied name you bear, nor what a filthy burden is bound to you.' (p.356)

Unlike the other characters, Jane and Rochester are bound by their experiences of overwhelming and clashing emotions.

# Rebellion and revenge

One of the novel's most revealing scenes is Mrs Reed's reaction to Jane's outburst after she is locked in the Red Room:

> 'I am glad you are no relation of mine. I will never call you aunt again as long as I live. I will never come to see you when I am grown up; and if anyone asks me how I liked you, and how you treated me, I will say the very thought of you makes me sick, and that you treated me with miserable cruelty.' (p.44)

Rejecting all the rules of 'correct' female conduct, Jane relentlessly challenges her oppressors. Jane's behaviour can be interpreted as 'masculine' – especially in early life, when she uses violence to get her way with John Reed.

Later, though, Jane develops more subtle methods of rebellion, increasingly defending herself verbally rather than physically.

The flip side of the positive impulse of rebellion is the negative impulse of revenge. Here, it is possible to interpret *Jane Eyre* as a rather less benign novel than it at first seems. It is true that the main character is admirable – but how much do we know about her?

As discussed earlier, the punishments received by characters in the novel are oddly proportional to the level of pain that they have inflicted on Jane. People who severely hurt Jane are punished, while people who help her are rewarded: Brocklehurst is disgraced, John Reed is killed after being thrown from a horse, Rochester is disfigured, Mrs Reed dies embittered. In this sense, the plot of *Jane Eyre* works as an effective mechanism for Jane's revenge.

## Racism

As the character of Bertha suggests, there is a parallel between the situation of dominated women and that of the victims of British Colonialism. While it is ambiguous whether *Jane Eyre* advocates the idea of racial superiority, it is obvious that Bertha is unjustly treated. Kept cooped up like a degenerate animal, the mentally ill Bertha is victimised by British society.

In *Wide Sargasso Sea*, Jean Rhys re-imagines Rochester's first marriage from Bertha's point of view, making her into a far more sympathetic character. For Rhys, madness and the effects of racial tension are inextricably combined.

Brontë treats the issue of race quite traditionally. Although Jane does express some sympathy toward Bertha, even protesting to Rochester that 'she cannot help being mad' (p.347), this unfortunate person is treated in the novel as an obstacle to be overcome. Her 'madness' is never really dealt with adequately, and she is mostly a passive victim of her circumstances. Jane's residual sympathy for Bertha is eventually overcome by her instinctive sense of superiority.

## Natural versus institutionalised religion

The role of religion in the novel is quite complex. Brontë, of course, was writing in a society that was considerably more religious than our own. Her father was a minister, and she was highly familiar with church ritual and scripture.

It is strange, therefore, that *Jane Eyre* can be seen as a rejection of conventional religion. The main representatives of religion in the novel – Mr Brocklehurst and St John Rivers – are both extremely dominating, misogynist figures (i.e. they both hate or belittle women). Brontë sees their hatred of women and sexuality as the central flaw in traditional religion.

However, Brontë does not reject *all* religion. In fact, *Jane Eyre* can be seen as Brontë's attempt to construct a more natural and 'human' version of religious belief. This radicalism is revealed in Jane's negative reaction to Helen's idea of the afterlife:

> 'And shall I see you again, Helen, when I die?'
>
> 'You will come to the same region of happiness: be received by the same mighty, universal Parent, no doubt, dear Jane.'
>
> Again I questioned, but this time only in thought. 'Where is that region? Does it exist?' (p.97)

Unlike Helen's, Jane's God is *not* disembodied and supernatural. Instead, Jane believes in an earthly God, not an abstracted heavenly one. *Jane Eyre* therefore represents traditional Christianity as a destructive force. Later, grappling with her love for Rochester, Jane again elaborates on her relationship with God, eventually deciding to 'keep the law given by God, sanctioned by man' (p.362). Yet her subversive vision of God would be unrecognisable to someone like Brocklehurst. (Note, though, that he hypocritically fails to apply his strict standards to his own daughters, who wear 'grey beaver hats, then in fashion, shaded with ostrich plumes, and from under the brim of this graceful head-dress fell a profusion of light tresses, elaborately curled' (p.77).

The book was heavily criticised on its release for its immorality. To many, Jane's creation of a kind of 'natural religion' seemed uncomfortably close to 'animism', i.e. to the practice of endowing physical objects with spiritual essences. Although she often refers to 'God', the church fathers of Jane's day would not have approved of her interpretation of

Christianity. By placing the individual, rather than God, in the centre of her world, *Jane Eyre* convincingly argues for a more human and inclusive religion than the one dominant in England and Europe at the time.

## Fairy tales and fantasy

There are multiple fairy tales embedded in *Jane Eyre*'s narrative, the most famous being the legend of Bluebeard, who was said to have kept the body of his many murdered wives in a locked room. In some ways, Rochester resembles this character.

The original fairy tales are far more disturbing than the modern 'Disney' versions we are now accustomed to. Many are explicitly concerned with sexuality, and feature monstrous male figures such as Rumplestiltskin, who lust after the pure and innocent heroine.

The language of fantasy and fairy tales is used often in *Jane Eyre*. Rochester calls Jane 'fairy-born and human bred' (p.505), and she bears a superficial resemblance to the 'damsel in distress'. Likewise, Rochester is frequently compared to ogre-type beings such as 'the evil-spirited Gytrash' – an archaic word for a monstrous creature.

However, the novel also heavily criticises fairy-tale ideals: Rochester's habit of referring to Jane as a 'fairy' or a 'changeling' is designed to keep her in her place. By rejecting the passive fairy-tale ideal of women, Jane demands instead to be seen as fully human.

The 'fairy-tale' ideal of femininity is still with us. Journalist Sushi Das recently argued that the obsession with 'Fairies, princesses, angels, and ballerinas ... encourages ideas of women as passive objects of admiration' (*The Age,* 2010), and Jane's rejection of superficiality makes precisely the same point.

## Homelessness and alienation

Because Jane eventually finds true love and friendship, it's easy to forget her loneliness. Bessie's childhood song 'The poor orphan child' refers to Jane's isolation.

> There is a thought that for strength should avail me;
> Though both of shelter and kindred despoiled;
> Heaven is a home, and a rest will not fail me;
> God is a friend to the poor orphan child. (p.27)

Jane's journeys through the novel's major locations – Gateshead, Lowood, Thornfield, Marsh End and Ferndean – can be seen as a quest for 'belonging'. Virtually every location in which Jane finds herself is unsatisfactory, and only Ferndean's peaceful surroundings can finally provide her with a true home.

Jane frequently experiences alienation. Living with Mrs Reed, she is never made 'part of the family'. Similarly, at Lowood, Jane is reduced to a cog in a machine, where each girl is seen as a potential source of evil. At Thornfield, she is still not 'at home' in the traditional sense: Brocklehurst's dominating nature prevents her from feeling truly welcome.

Finally, at Millcote, Jane seems to find a place in which she is comfortable. 'My home ... is a cottage; a little room with white-washed walls and a sanded floor' (p.413), she contentedly remarks. After discovering her relatives, Jane comments:

> 'And you ... cannot at all imagine the craving I have for fraternal and sisterly love. I never had a home, I never had brothers or sisters; I must and will have them now ...' (p.447)

However, St John's imperious (dominating) nature still prevents Jane from feeling at home in this otherwise congenial (welcoming) environment – something which is only provided by the modest surroundings of Ferndean.

## Class

While the novel does not talk explicitly about class, the issue is often dealt with indirectly. Jane has no money, and she is never allowed to forget this. John Reed, for example, insists that Jane call him 'Master Reed' – a mark of his superior financial status. Miss Abbot warns Jane that 'you ought not to think yourself on an equality with the Misses Reed and Master Reed ... it is your place to be humble' (p.16). It is precisely this demand of humility and subservience that Jane rejects.

Yet interestingly, the novel does not really argue that poor and rich should be treated equally. Jane receives a substantial inheritance, thereby immediately elevating her to the upper-middle class. Even after her decision to give away three-quarters of her fortune to her relatives, she is still positioned substantially above the masses. Early in life, in fact, Jane admits that she 'should not like to belong to poor people' (p.30).

The discovery of Jane's inheritance reflects a Victorian association between virtue and class. Many Victorian novels end with a poor central character receiving a large inheritance, which supports the idea that people will eventually get the wealth they 'deserve'.

## Original Sin

The doctrine of Original Sin was – and in many cases still is – a central theme of the Christian religion. According to this idea, man (and woman) was born into a 'fallen state', i.e. they are corrupted from birth and must be redeemed through good deeds on Earth. According to the Bible, this 'fallen' state of humanity originated when Adam and Eve ate from the 'tree of knowledge' in the Garden of Eden. Adam and Eve suddenly become aware of their nakedness after doing so, and seek to cover themselves up before God, who is furious at their transgression (misdeed):

> And he said, Who told thee that thou *wast* naked? Hast thou eaten of the tree, whereof I commanded thee thou shouldest not eat? (Genesis 3:11)

The doctrine of Original Sin has historically been used to portray women as inherently sinful beings, capable of morally corrupting men. By displaying hubris (Godlike ambition), humanity became 'fallen' in the eyes of God, an idea which inspired the common association between sin and sexuality.

St John is the novel's main representative of this idea. He crushes his attraction to Miss Olivier, who has 'a face of perfect beauty' (p.418), admitting that 'I rested my temples on the breast of temptation' (p.430). For St John, Miss Oliver is a temptress whose 'promises are hollow' (p.430). St John sees sexuality as a dangerously corrupting force that must be banished from the soul.

Yet *Jane Eyre* rejects the doctrine of Original Sin by exalting Jane's desire for Rochester. While a modern audience may find Brontë's cautious attitude toward the subject difficult to understand, it is important to remember that it was deemed morally unacceptable for women to sleep with men outside of marriage in nineteenth-century England. By embracing desire, rather than seeing it as evidence of sinfulness, Jane firmly opposes the Christian doctrine of her day.

# Redemption

Although Jane remains as true to herself in adulthood as she was in childhood, *Jane Eyre* also contains the story of Rochester's painful and gradual redemption.

Rochester is, by his own admission, an extremely flawed figure. Although his marriage to Bertha makes it legally impossible for him to marry Jane, his ethical laxity makes this equally unlikely. Jane is 'too good' for Rochester and considers herself to be so – an unusual position to take in an age where rich men could usually take their pick of women. Jane's *character*, not her material wealth, places her above Rochester, and the two cannot be permanently united until Rochester is thoroughly reformed.

By narrating his life story, Rochester treats Jane as a 'confessional' to whom he can use to expiate (dissolve) his guilt. But these confessions are not enough: his behaviour must also change before Jane's mind and heart can be won over.

The injuries suffered by Rochester steer him off the path of immorality that Jane detests. The Rochester that Jane marries at the end of the novel is therefore a very different person that the one she fell in love with: by becoming both humble and faithful, Rochester finally emerges victorious over his desires.

Jane does not require similar redemption, because the narrator always describes her behaviour as fully justified. Jane always 'stands up for what is right', even if this results in serious consequences. This distinguishes *Jane Eyre* from a more typical *Bildungsroman*, in which the protagonist must recognise and overcome his or her faults before entering adulthood.

# DIFFERENT INTERPRETATIONS

Different interpretations arise from different responses to a text. Over time, a text will give rise to a wide range of responses from its readers, who may come from various social or cultural groups and live in very different places and historical periods. These responses can be published in newspapers, journals and books by critics and reviewers, or they can be expressed in discussions among readers in the media, classrooms, book groups and so on. While there is no single correct reading or interpretation of a text, it is important to understand that an interpretation is more than an 'opinion' – it is the justification of a point of view on the text. To present an interpretation of the text based on your point of view you must use a logical argument and support it with relevant evidence from the text.

## Feminist interpretations

Most critics acknowledge *Jane Eyre*'s role as a central novel of feminism. To understand the extent to which Brontë was challenging the dominant ideals of her day, it is important to remember the different attitudes over the past century and a half. Female conformity was expected; wives were seen as the property of their husbands, and had few or no rights within the family. Women were expected to be obedient and passive, unsuited to public life or deep thought.

By relentlessly attacking the hypocrisy of the male-dominated society, Charlotte Brontë was a key force in loosening the strictures that surrounded the women of her day. Although we think of the nineteenth century as a reactionary time, gender divisions were gradually being challenged in Brontë's England: the country had a powerful and admired queen (Victoria), and the legal system was gradually granting increased freedoms to women.

Critics draw attention to the uniquely feminine nature of Brontë's writing. For example, Adrienne Rich has noticed the inclusion of 'a young woman of strong sensuality' (2001, p.475), while Sandra Gilbert claims that Jane's dealings with Rochester constitute 'political rather than sexual statements' (2001, p.486). Both of these critics explicitly position *Jane Eyre* as a central feminist text.

## Humanist interpretations

While this gender-based idea is obviously a major theme of the novel, other critics have sought to define Jane's struggle more generally. Jerome Beaty, for example, notes that the novel is often interpreted as an account of 'the legitimate assertion of the sovereignty of the self' (2001, p.491). Central to this reading – and also linking it to the feminist reading of the novel as an assertion of sexual equality – is the central role of desire in Jane's humanist vision. While St John's 'path to salvation lies through self-denial … Jane's … lies through everyday, domestic life, the path of *eros*' (pp.499–500).

In many ways, these readings are interdependent. Jane's story is female, yes, but it is not *only* female – it is also human. Jane's growth links her with the wider human experience: her story is universal.

## *Jane Eyre* as a love story

Of course, *Jane Eyre* is also one of the most affecting love stories in English Literature. The tale has all the characteristics of a 'Mills and Boon'-type romance: a timid heroine, a brooding hero, a competing lover, a dark secret, and most importantly, a happy ending. For instance, Cynthia Carlton-Ford sees the novel as Jane's quest to be able to solve the classic Romantic dilemma of how to get 'close enough for intimacy, yet far enough away for some degree of autonomy' (2001, p.350).

The archetypal love story can be defined as 'boy meets girl' (part 1), boy loses girl' (part 2), and 'boy gets girl again' (part 3). When these elements are taken at face value, *Jane Eyre* becomes the most traditional of romances. It differs from more conventional examples, however, in the unusually high level of independence granted to its forthright female protagonist.

## *Jane Eyre* as a celebration of childhood

However appealing the elder Jane may be, the young Jane is more memorable. As in many novels, the spontaneous, exuberant voice of childhood is more appealing than the tamed, restricted voice of adulthood. Stevie Davies points out in his introduction to the novel, 'the child's visceral intensity still informs the tongue of the woman' (2006, p.xxxi).

Something about the young Jane is indeed unusually appealing. Her earlier self acts with such a sense of spontaneity that the reader is carried along with her enthusiasm. As Richard Benvenuto notes, 'What Jane is, in her innate self, is right' (1996, p.215).

There is also a particular sense of immediacy about the young Jane. Whereas the older narrator sees the world in a more complex and qualified way, the young character is pure passion. When narrating the child's story, the elder Jane temporarily becomes 'swept up' in the power of the child's voice. Jane ends the novel as a respectable adult, but her actions as an incorrigible child have a lasting impact.

This preference for the child's perspective signifies the book's status as a Romantic classic. The Brontës were followers of the poet William Wordsworth, who was partly responsible for changing how people thought about childhood. In his *Ode to Immortality*, he writes:

> ... and not in utter nakedness,
> But trailing clouds of glory do we come
> From God, who is our home:
> Heaven lies about us in our infancy! (1804, lines 64–67)

Wordsworth's attitude toward childhood was revolutionary. Before the Romantic movement, many children were not considered as beings worthy of separate consideration, being instead viewed as 'potential adults'. Wordsworth and his contemporaries helped introduce the idea of childhood as a uniquely blessed time, which only becomes corrupted during adulthood: the opposite of the 'Original Sin' doctrine.

Seeing childhood as a uniquely enlightened state is central to Brontë's vision. The young Jane may not know how to act around others, but her reactions to her harsh treatment are always shown to be *right*. It is always adults, and not the children, who are corrupt.

## Gothic interpretations

Several critics have observed the Gothic parallels between the demonic character of Bertha and that of Jane. Lisa Sternlieb, for example, notes that 'Bertha's demonic malignity is consistently followed by Jane's exaggerated benignity', as 'Jane uses Bertha's attacks to advertise her own utter harmlessness' (2001, p.509).

According to Sternlieb, though, this apparent harmlessness is a ruse. Jane's 'own revenge is successful because it is everything Bertha's is not – controlled, sustained, articulate, and above all, disguised' (p.510). By concealing her hostile attitude toward others, Jane is able to manipulate others without being detected.

This revenge narrative is closely bound up with the idea that Jane, as the narrator, has a huge amount of power over the *reader*, who is 'repeatedly pitted against Rochester for Jane's affections' (p.513). Jane's hold over the reader relies on her concealment of her 'monstrous' nature, which allows her to get away with far more than a less-sympathetic character would.

## Marxist interpretations

One of the most prominent aspects of the novel is its condemnation of England's class system at the time, which Brontë saw as inherently corrupt and enabling the oppression of other, less-powerful characters. Critic Charlie Smith, for example, argues that Jane's enemies 'are doomed by their environments established by class division' (Smith 2006).

It is debatable, however, how much the novel can be interpreted as an overall attack on the class system itself. Jane, after all, becomes happy after she has inherited enough money to buy her escape from the punishing world in which she grew up; although she reminds us that poverty is not the same as lack of virtue, it is equally important that she does everything she can to get out of the underclass.

## Two contrasting interpretations

Any text is open to contrasting, yet equally valid, interpretations. Presented below are two different ways of interpreting the novel.

**1. *Jane Eyre* is a conventional novel of development about a girl's growth into a young woman.**
The narrative of *Jane Eyre*, when seen in a linear way, is a collection of traditional events. Jane's life story describes her path to domestic conformity. While she does demonstrate some rebellious instincts in her early life, these are gradually leached away until we are left with a conventional, unexceptional woman whose greatest wish is to settle down with a good husband and have a family. Jane does precisely this in the end – so despite her 'struggle' with Rochester and the other dominating men in her life, Jane succumbs to the pressure to conform.

By creating a character that temporarily resists the patriarchal order before eventually succumbing to it, Brontë has granted the status quo of her day a huge favour. Readers of the novel will witness a story of an unruly girl who eventually learned to behave 'properly' in her society; only after conforming to society's expectation of marriage does she finally achieve her goal of happiness.

Brontë seems unable to consider a viable alternative to conventional marriage, and her writing suffers for this. After spending most of her life rebelling, Jane is left with nowhere to go when she is finally permitted to sweep Rochester off his feet. It is true that he has lost his physical power, yet by creating a marriage with Jane, he is able to rid her of all the power that she once had.

Jane's early rebellions bring her nothing but trouble, while her later acceptance of her fate adds to her position within society. While Jane may have chosen a slightly unconventional husband for herself, she simply ends up like all the women around her. *Jane Eyre*, therefore, betrays the rebellious nature of its early sections in order to conform to social norms.

**2. *Jane Eyre* is a highly unconventional story of a character aggressively achieving dominance over all who challenge her.**

Although Jane enters a conventional marriage at the end of the novel, in fact there is nothing at all conventional about her story. From childhood, Jane seeks to challenge the authority of others, and just because her methods of doing this change doesn't mean that she stops when she reaches adulthood.

Those who find Jane's actions too restrained for their tastes should remember that Jane the *character* acts in concert with Jane the *narrator*. It is the narrator's role to maintain Jane's status as an underdog character, even when the odds fall overwhelmingly in her favour. Because Jane the narrator has total control over the novel's plot, she is able to structure events to her advantage.

Jane does not calm down or lose her passion as she grows older; instead, she just gets better at manipulating others and getting her own way. Notice how nobody crosses Jane and gets away with it – a reality that is only made possible by her brilliant manipulation of other characters' opinions of her to her favour.

Brontë has created a novel in which every possible element combines to assist the heroine in her journey. The narrative arcs of other characters are structured around Jane, and everyone else in the book is forced to respect her wishes.

# QUESTIONS & ANSWERS

## Essay writing: an overview

An essay is a formal and serious piece of writing that presents your point of view on the text, usually in response to a given essay topic. Your 'point of view' in an essay is your interpretation of the meaning of the text's language, structure, characters, situations and events, supported by detailed analysis of textual evidence.

### Analyse – don't summarise

In your essays it is important to avoid simply summarising what happens in a text:

- A **summary** is a description or paraphrase (retelling in different words) of the characters and events. For example: 'Macbeth has a horrifying vision of a dagger dripping with blood before he goes to murder King Duncan'.

- An **analysis** is an explanation of the real meaning or significance that lies 'beneath' the text's words (and images, for a film). For example: 'Macbeth's vision of a bloody dagger shows how deeply uneasy he is about the violent act he is contemplating – as well as his sense that supernatural forces are impelling him to act'.

A limited amount of summary is sometimes necessary to let your reader know which part of the text you wish to discuss. However, always keep this to a minimum and follow it immediately with your analysis (explanation) of what this part of the text is really telling us.

### Plan your essay

Carefully plan your essay so that you have a clear idea of what you are going to say. The plan ensures that your ideas flow logically, that your argument remains consistent and that you stay on the topic. An essay plan should be a list of **brief dot points** – no more than half a page. It includes:

- your central argument or main contention – a concise statement (usually in a single sentence) of your overall response to the topic. See 'Analysing a sample topic' for guidelines on how to formulate a main contention.

- three or four dot points for each paragraph indicating the main idea and evidence/examples from the text. Note that in your essay you will need to *expand* on these points and *analyse* the evidence.

## Structure your essay

An essay is a complete, self-contained piece of writing. It has a clear beginning (the introduction), middle (several body paragraphs) and end (the last paragraph or conclusion). It must also have a central argument that runs throughout, linking each paragraph to form a coherent whole.

See examples of introductions and conclusions in the 'Analysing a sample topic' and 'Sample answer' sections.

**The introduction establishes your overall response to the topic.** It includes your main contention and outlines the main evidence you will refer to in the course of the essay. Write your introduction *after* you have done a plan and *before* you write the rest of the essay.

**The body paragraphs argue your case** – they present evidence from the text and explain how this evidence supports your argument. Each body paragraph needs:

- a strong **topic sentence** (usually the first sentence) that states the main point being made in the paragraph
- **evidence** from the text, including some brief quotations
- **analysis** of the textual evidence explaining its significance and **explanation** of how it supports your argument
- **links back to the topic** in one or more statements, usually towards the end of the paragraph.

Connect the body paragraphs so that your discussion flows smoothly. Use some linking words and phrases like 'similarly' and 'on the other hand', but don't start every paragraph like this. Another strategy is to use a significant word from the last sentence of one paragraph in the first sentence of the next.

Use key terms from the topic – or similes for them – throughout, so the relevance of your discussion to the topic is always clear.

**The conclusion ties everything together and finishes the essay.** It includes strong statements that emphasise your central argument and provide a clear response to the topic.

Avoid simply restating the points made earlier in the essay – this will end on a very flat note and imply that you have run out of ideas and vocabulary. The conclusion is meant to be a logical extension of what you have written, rather than a repetition or summary of it. Writing an effective conclusion can be a challenge. Try using these tips:

- Start by linking back to the final sentence of the second-last paragraph – this helps your writing to 'flow', rather than just leaping back to your main contention straight away.

- Use similes and expressions with equivalent meanings to vary your vocabulary. This allows you to reinforce your line of argument without being repetitive.

- When planning your essay, think of one or two broad statements or observations about the text's wider meaning. These should be related to the topic and your overall argument. Keep them for the conclusion, since they will give you something 'new' to say but still follow logically from your discussion. The introduction will be focused on the topic, but the conclusion can present a wider view of the text.

## Sample essay topics

1   'Although Jane initially seems like a benign character, she is in fact highly aggressive and always gets her own way.' Do you agree?

2   'The treatment of Bertha in *Jane Eyre* suggests a disturbing lack of compassion for the disadvantaged.' Discuss.

3   What do Jane's struggles with St John and Rochester reveal about her personality?

4   'Jane made the wrong decision not to become Rochester's mistress.' Do you agree?

5   How does Jane's rejection of traditional religion affect her actions?

6   'Jane is the novel's only complex and believable character. All the rest are stereotypes.' Discuss.

7   Does St John have any redeeming features?

8   '*Jane Eyre* is a feminist novel far ahead of its time.' Do you agree?

9   'By eventually agreeing to marry Rochester, Jane needlessly sacrifices her hard-won independence.' Do you agree?

10  'By providing Jane with a large fortune, Bronte destroys the novel's powerful critique of the class system.' Discuss.

# Useful vocabulary for writing on this text

*Bildungsroman* – a 'novel of development', in which the character grows throughout the course of the story.

**Feminism** – a movement focused on achieving equality for women in patriarchal (male-dominated) societies. *Jane Eyre* can be seen as a feminist novel due to its compelling and independent heroine.

**Gothic** – a literary and artistic movement that reached its height in the late-eighteenth and early-nineteenth centuries. Focusing on mental instability, personal fragmentation, fear, paranoia, danger and despair, the deeply pessimistic Gothic movement viewed the individual as dark and unknowable. Its common visual motifs included haunted houses, strangers with dark secrets, and death-related imagery.

**Realist novel** – a narrative form that includes significant amounts of realistic description about the physical environment.

**Romanticism** – a literary, artistic and philosophical movement that flourished in England in the early to mid-nineteenth century, which saw humanity – rather than God – as the source of meaning.

## Sample analysis of a topic

**'By eventually agreeing to marry Rochester, Jane needlessly sacrifices all her hard-won independence.' Do you agree?**

This question asks you to analyse Jane's character. To do this, you will have to decide whether she has remained true to her original vision, or whether her final decision makes her earlier struggles meaningless.

The most logical place to start would be to look at the question's *premise*, i.e. the key assumptions that it is making. For example, this question implies that Jane had achieved a high level of independence before marrying Rochester. Is this true? You will have to find out by looking back at the major events in her life, and evaluating whether or not these actually increased her independence.

As the book is too long and complex to revise Jane's *entire* life story, it would be better to isolate a few key moments in her long struggle for independence. For example, you could look at her victories over John and Mrs Reed, along with her (small) retaliation against Brocklehurst and her rejection of both St John and Rochester. In each case, Jane *does* gain an increased level of independence. These three events seem to prove beyond doubt that Jane is a person of very strong will; however, you will have to argue this case in your essay by using evidence.

Next, look specifically at the other part of the question: Jane's marriage to Rochester. What is the nature of this marriage? Is it different to his original proposal? To find this out, you will have to look at how Rochester's character has changed.

Comparing the Rochester of the first proposal to the Rochester of the second, we can see some clear differences. For example, while the original Rochester is arrogant, sexist and dominating, the later Rochester seems humble, reserved and compassionate. Thinking about how this change in his character might affect the nature of their eventual marriage could be helpful in understanding the changes that have occurred.

Now, think about the 'Jane' part of the equation. What is the question implying? It seems to say that Jane has betrayed her core principles by marrying Rochester and taking up a conventional existence. Is this true?

While it could be argued that Jane shouldn't settle for anyone else, that is not what she has expressed throughout her life. Instead, she has consistently reminded the reader of her need for love and companionship, and has demonstrated her love for Rochester. Of course, marriage always involves the loss of *some* independence – but seeing this as a bad thing doesn't seem justified in Jane's case. She has always been clear about her willingness to give up her isolation for the right person.

A second possibility arises, though: what if Rochester is not good enough for Jane? That would explain the word 'needlessly', because it suggests that Jane would be 'throwing herself away' on him. Has Rochester proved himself worthy of Jane, or is he still relatively unchanged?

To answer this, you will have to look at the suffering that Rochester has gone through, and at how his character has changed since the catastrophic events at Thornfield. You could either argue that Rochester has not redeemed himself sufficiently, or that he has. Either way, you will have to use evidence of the changes that take place in Rochester's behaviour over time to justify your argument.

# SAMPLE ANSWER

**'Although Jane initially seems like a benign character, she is in fact highly aggressive toward others.' Do you agree?**

On the surface, the protagonist of Charlotte Brontë's *Jane Eyre* seems like a positive character; yet she is more aggressive than she appears. From early childhood onward, Jane demonstrates the will and the ability to defend herself against some powerful and aggressive people, as her first confrontation with the brutal John Reed shows:

> He ran headlong at me: I felt him grasp my hair and my shoulder: he had closed with a desperate thing ... he called me 'Rat! rat!' and bellowed out aloud. (p.9)

After Jane is severely punished by her cold and controlling guardian, Mrs Reed, she is utterly unrepentant. Expecting an apology, the shocked Mrs Reed instead hears the words: 'I will never call you aunt again as long as I live.' (p.44)

The adult male characters try even harder to force Jane to comply to an unthreatening stereotype of passive femininity. She refuses. One of the most interesting ways in which she is able to stand up to people far more powerful than her is through ridicule and parody. For example, Jane describes the malevolent Brocklehurst as a 'black pillar' with a head like a 'carved mask' (p.26), and a heart 'made up of equal parts of whalebone and iron' (p.86). These harsh descriptions make Brocklehurst seem even more unsympathetic to the reader than he is already. Later on, Brocklehurst is disgraced when his school's brutal treatment of students is exposed. Jane doesn't cause this directly, but the exposure plays right into her hands. After this, Brocklehurst ceases to be a credible foe. Even as Jane grows as a person after each successive victory over her foes, her habit of playing the 'underdog' makes her dominating nature easy to overlook.

The other male characters' clumsy attempts to dominate Jane fall flat, even if they initially seem likely to succeed. Rochester, for example, is a more subtle agent of patriarchy than Brocklehurst, because he is both Jane's love interest and her oppressor. Yet he presents Jane with a bigger challenge than Brocklehurst's direct menace. Rochester is not overtly aggressive towards Jane, but he often objectifies her in sexist terms:

> You are a beauty, in my eyes; and a beauty just after the desire of my heart, – delicate and aërial. (p.299)

While Rochester tries to paint Jane as the passive female which she definitely is not, Jane won't accept such labelling. As she tells him, 'I am not an angel ... and I will not be one till I die: I will be myself' (p.300). When belittling Jane doesn't work, Rochester tries to put his own words in her mouth: when she announces her plans to leave him (p.350), Rochester comically replies: 'I pass over the madness about parting from me. You mean you must become a part of me' (p.350). But that doesn't work either: Jane departs for Whitcross soon after, despite Rochester's protestations. She is her own person, and no amount of trickery can convince her otherwise.

This isn't the only trick up Rochester's sleeve: he has previously resorted to disguising himself as a fortune-teller in order to extract information from Jane. Initially, this gives Rochester the upper hand in the relationship. The fortune-teller's arrival puts Jane into 'a kind of dream' (p.231) during which she lets her guard down and becomes 'involved in a web of mystification' (p.231). Unlike the self-contained dreamlike fantasies which Jane uses throughout her life as a means of escape, her temporary lapse gives Rochester power over her, which disappears when he is forced to reveal his identity.

For someone so closely matched with Jane, Rochester can be surprisingly inept, virtually a figure of fun. His confident but misguided observations are either misogynistic ('The passions may rage furiously' (p.233)); wishful ('Mademoiselle is a fairy' (p.309)); or clueless ('Did you expect a present, Miss Eyre? Are you fond of presents?' (p.142)). Rochester's attempts to assert power over Jane become increasingly ridiculous as his authority over her crumbles, and he only begins his rehabilitation as a character after he learns to accept his limitations.

St John is the text's most formidable male – even more so than Rochester, who lacks his pure power. Yet even this is not enough to tame Jane in the end. While St John's attacks on Jane's right to assert herself are far more subtle than Rochester's, they draw on the same impulse: domination of women. Issuing an ultimatum to Jane, St John asks her to:

> Simplify your complicated interests, feelings, thoughts, wishes, aims; merge all considerations in one purpose: that of fulfilling with effect – with power – the mission of your great Master.
> (p.468)

Although St John is talking about Christ here, he may just as well be talking about himself. St John is a much greater threat to Jane than Rochester is, because his superficially 'feminine' aspects conceal his essentially masculine nature. Yet even in the face of this blatant force, Jane finds the strength to resist him.

The seemingly insignificant figure of Jane often seems to be utterly overwhelmed by her opponents, yet she always manages to use a combination of sheer will and cleverness to overcome their many pressure tactics. While the novel's more overtly powerful characters attack her, they break rather than bend. Jane, the flexible and ingenious heroine, gets the upper hand every time.

# REFERENCES & READING

## Text

Brontë, Charlotte 2006 [1857] *Jane Eyre*, Penguin Classics, London.

## References

Alexander, Christine 2005, 'Preface', in Brontë, Charlotte 2005, *Tales of the Islanders: Volume 4*, edited by Christine Alexander and others, The Juvenilia Press, Sydney, pp.viii–xviii.

Austen, Jane 2002 [1813] *Pride and Prejudice*, Penguin Classics, London.

Baldick, Chris 1992, 'Introduction', in *The Oxford Book of Gothic Tales*, Oxford University Press, Oxford, pp. xi–xxiii.

Beaty, Jerome 2001, 'St John's Way and the Wayward Reader', in *Jane Eyre: Norton Critical Edition*, WW Norton & Company, New York, pp.491–503.

Benvenuto, Richard 1996, 'The Child of Nature, the Child of Grace, and the Unresolved Conflict of *Jane Eyre*', in McNees, Eleanor (ed.), *The Brontë Sisters: Critical Assessments*, East Sussex, Helm Information, pp.210–225.

Brontë, Charlotte 2001 [1836], 'All this day I have been in a dream', in *Jane Eyre: Norton Critical Edition*, W W Norton & Company, New York, pp.403–406.

Brontë, Charlotte 1985 [1853] *Villette*, Penguin Classics, London.

Bunyan, John 2010 [1678] *The Pilgrim's Progress*, Penguin Classics, London.

Carlton-Ford, Cynthia, 'Intimacy Without Immolation: Fire in *Jane Eyre*', in McNees, Eleanor (ed.), *The Brontë Sisters: Critical Assessments*, East Sussex, Helm Information, pp.342–351.

Das, Sushi 2010, 'Pink deluge a lesson in inequality', *The Age*, 20 December 2010, http://www.theage.com.au/opinion/politics/pink-deluge-a-lesson-in-inequality-20101220-19258.html, accessed 4 January 2010.

Davies, Stevie 2006, 'Introduction', in Charlotte Brontë, *Jane Eyre*, Penguin Classics, London, pp.xi–xlii.

Dickens, Charles 1985 [1849–50] *David Copperfield*, Penguin Classics, London.

Dickens, Charles 1996 [1860–61] *Great Expectations*, Penguin Classics, London.

Dickens, Charles 2008 [1838–9] *Nicholas Nickleby*, Kindle Edition.

Freud, Sigmund 1909, 'Family Romances', *The Adoption History Project*, http://darkwing.uoregon.edu/~adoption/archive/FreudFR. htm, accessed 4 January 2010.

Gilbert, Sandra 2001, 'A Dialogue of Self and Soul: Plain Jane's Progress', in *Jane Eyre: Norton Critical Edition*, WW Norton & Co., New York, pp.483–491.

Gilbert, Sandra and Susan Gubar 1984, *The Madwoman in the Attic*, New Haven, Yale University Press.

Jackson, Mark 1996, 'Fairy Tales in *Alice in Wonderland* and *Jane Eyre*', *The Victorian Web*, http://www.victorianweb.org/authors/Brontë/ cBrontë/73cbfairy.html, accessed 4 January 2010.

Rich, Adrienne 2001, 'Jane Eyre: the Temptations of a Motherless Woman', in *Jane Eyre: Norton Critical Edition*, WW Norton & Co., New York, pp.469–483.

Rhys, Jean 1979 [1966], *Wide Sargasso Sea*, Penguin, London.

Shakespeare, William 1998 [c.1596–8] 'The Merchant of Venice', in *The Oxford Shakespeare: The Complete Works*, Clarendon Press, Oxford, pp.426–451.

Showalter, Elaine 1977 *A Literature of Their Own: British women novelists from Brontë to Lessing*, Virago, London.

Smith, Charlie 2006, *The Jane Eyre Manifesto: A Marxist Hero for the British Empire*, http://www.associatedcontent.com/article/104238/the_ jane_eyre_manifesto_a_marxist_hero.html, accessed 14 January 2011.

Sternlieb, Lisa 2001, 'Jane Eyre: Hazarding Confidences', in *Jane Eyre: Norton Critical Edition*, WW Norton & Co, New York, pp. 503–515.

Stevenson, Robert Lois 2003 [1886] *The Strange Case of Dr Jekyll and Mr Hyde*, Penguin Classics, London.

Wordsworth, William 1804, *Intimations of Immortality*, http://www. bartleby.com/101/536.html, accessed 13 January 2010.

# notes

notes

# notes

# notes

[2]

CPSIA information can be obtained at www.ICGtesting.com
Printed in the USA
LVOW071437231212

312975LV00001B/126/P

9 781921 411847